Useful Questions

A Guide to Self-Coaching

??????? ?

CORRINN R. DAVIS

WHISTLING
RABBIT
PRESS

Contact the publisher at info@whistlingrabbitpress.com
Contact the author at the website www.citstation.com

A portion of the proceeds from sales of this book will benefit the CALROCK Ranch for sex trafficking survivors.

Paperback ISBN: 978-1-950835-01-0
eBook ISBN: 978-1-950835-02-7

> Publisher's Cataloging-in-Publication Data
> Names: Davis, Corrinn, R., author.
> Title: Useful questions : a guide to self-coaching / Corrinn R. Davis.
> Description: San Diego, CA: Whistling Rabbit Press, 2020.
> Identifiers: LCCN:2019954646 | ISBN: 978-1-950835-01-0 (pbk.) | 978-1-950835-01-0 (ebook)
> Subjects: LCSH Self-talk. | Change (Psychology) | Self-actualization (Psychology). | Happiness. | Conduct of life. | Self-esteem. | BISAC SELF-HELP / Personal Growth / General
> Classification: LCC BF637.C4 .D38 2019 | DDC 158.1--dc23

Cover design by **Victoria Davies at VC Book Cover Designs**
Interior design by **Arc Manor Book Design**

Published by
Whistling Rabbit Press
San Diego, California
whistlingrabbitpress.com

Printed in the United States of America

CONTENTS

ACKNOWLEDGMENTS

This book is a collection of decades of life experiences, lessons, and personal stories that have been influenced by and experienced with many. I am forever grateful to you all.

To my crazy-intense, ferociously loving family: You are and continue to be the crucible for many of my most important learnings. This ride with you has been a microcosm of the biggest challenges, the most fantastic joys, and the deepest love this life has to offer. "LYBM SMICSI"

To my incomparable friends: There really are no words to express the depth of my appreciation for you. Your value in my life is unsurpassed. You have been my champions, cheerleaders, and accountability partners. You have picked me up when I've been down, dusted me off, put me back together, and set me back on track. Every day, through your love and your shining examples, you call me to my highest and best. It is an honor and a privilege to share this journey with you.

To my exceptional mentors—some of whom I have never even met: Thank you, thank you, thank you for your generosity of spirit and for sharing your wisdom, insights, and love in ways that have immeasurably enriched my life. It will remain a lifelong goal to pay your kindness and generosity forward.

To my incredible publisher and editor: Without you, this book would never have come into being. Thank you for your belief in me, for the support you gave me, the structure you provided, and for your incredible generosity with all of your resources and your beautiful heart. I'm so glad we met and that you are in my life.

To my God: I would be remiss if I did not also acknowledge my deepest gratitude to You, without whom I literally cannot even take a breath. From You all goodness flows, and I have been blessed beyond measure by Your tender love and care. To You I owe all.

A deep and abiding thank you to each and every one of you who have touched my life in such profound ways. This book, and my life, are better for having the privilege of knowing you and/or being exposed to your teachings. May your roads be as rich as the one you have helped me forge.

INTRODUCTION

How This Book Came to Be

There were several hundred of us in the room, and you could have heard a pin drop. On carpet. It was day two of Jack Canfield's weeklong personal development seminar, and things were getting very intense. Jack had asked us at the beginning of the workshop to refrain from interrupting the process if anyone was going through a cathartic experience. We agreed we would not offer a tissue, a shoulder, or a hug, but would simply sit quietly and be mentally, emotionally, and spiritually present, to the best of our ability, while Jack guided the person through the beginning stages of their healing and evolution.

He had created a completely safe emotional space in a very short period of time. That blanket of loving safety allowed a 60-something-year-old woman I'll call Lisa to begin to recall, for the first time and in graphic detail, the brutal and repeated sexual molestations her father had perpetrated against her when she was a young girl. As she described the horror and trauma she had repeatedly endured as a child, this strong yet momentarily fragile woman kept asking through her sobs, "Why?" "Why would he do this to me?" "Why?"

With an expression of extreme tenderness and compassion, with all the brotherly love you can imagine, Jack looked into her eyes and said, "Lisa, sometimes *Why?* just isn't a **useful** question." The profundity of that statement nearly knocked me out of my chair. I then witnessed the raw power of the more useful questions he asked her and how they helped her begin to transcend the atrocities of her youth.

Jack's statement really stuck with me. *Why?* was the primary question of my life up to that point. If *Why?* wasn't a useful question, what was? And useful for what?

It would be many years, therapists, workshops, and coaches later, before all the pieces came together and the answers to those questions gelled.

The answer to the *Useful for what?* question was this: for creating breakthroughs; for becoming aware of limiting patterns; for healing past hurts; for processing difficult emotions; for getting unstuck; for taking action; for making a plan; for stepping out on a well-paved road or an unknown course; for transforming; for transcending; for crafting a better version of yourself and creating a better life.

In essence, a useful question is one that helps you move to the next level in your life—whatever that level is—to create a life you envision and a quality of experience you intend instead of just letting life happen to you like a fledgling bird being tossed about in a rain storm.

It occurred to me that journeys of exploration into the self and into the creation of your future **begin** with questions. I finally realized that every counselor or coach I'd ever had guided me further down the path of deeper understanding by using skillfully crafted and well-timed questions.

So I started looking at those questions—decades worth—and I noticed a few things. The first was that some of the questions kept showing up over and over again, sometimes verbatim, sometimes slightly changed, at different times and in different situations. Eventually, I came to understand that they were presented to me again if I hadn't understood the lesson, if I hadn't grasped a nuance from the first (or second or third) time the question presented itself, or if I hadn't begun to **live** the lesson. I was being given another chance to incorporate the gifts inherent in **asking** the question.

The second realization was that some of the questions tended to address or guide my way through specific topics such as coping with fear, acceptance, forgiveness, etc. They were more effective for a specific application while others were more general and broadly applicable.

And the third was that all the questions that have served me so well throughout my life, that I have learned from people I respect, are questions that anyone can ask. But it is extremely important to pay attention to the quality of the questions you ask because the better the questions and the more appropriate they are to the situation, the quicker and more durable the learning, the deeper the healing, the larger the transformation, and the more fulfilling the life. Everything starts with the question because the questions set the trajectory of your life. Master life strategist Tony Robbins says it best: "If you want a better quality life, ask yourself a better quality question."

The best way I've found to determine if the question you're asking yourself is a quality question is to check in with how it makes you feel. If you feel depleted in any sense, try to reframe the question. The feeling you have about the question itself can be used as a guide to identify whether it will serve you well, whether it is a **useful** question.

For example, if you ask the question *Why is everything always so hard for me?* you'll likely feel very differently than if you ask *What do I need to learn from these challenges* or *What skills can I acquire to make things go more easily?*

Don't get me wrong. I believe everyone can benefit by having a coach (which is why I became one). It is a real advantage to have someone who will hold the space for your dreams until they start coming to fruition, who will challenge you, hold you accountable when your words and behavior are not aligned, lift you up when you need a boost, help you discover your blind spots, help you find the holes in your development that may need filling, help you get unstuck, help you craft a plan to realize your full potential, and who will inspire you to the heights of your own personal greatness.

But for the times when a coach isn't available or accessible, this book and these questions are a tool for being your own coach. This is a guide to *self*-coaching. It is an amalgamation of many of the questions that have been asked of me throughout my life; the questions that have served me best in the recursive hunt that **is** the introspective journey. Of course, there are endless questions you can ask, and most of the questions here can be used at different times and for different effects.

But these are the questions that have helped me the most—allowed me to cope, become more self-aware, tackle hurdles, heal hurts, improve the quality of my life, set intentions, and pursue my dreams. I have made many mistakes in my life, and these questions have been the very backbone of course correction, healing and learning to thrive.

I hope that the questions will help you on your own journey and that, along the way, you will begin to craft more questions for yourself in ways that will best serve you. To that end, let us begin.

How to Use This Book

First, let me say that using these questions (or anything else that facilitates the serious introspection that leads to a fulfilling, satisfying, rich experience of life) is **work**. Especially in the beginning. But if you can hold the value of the process in your mind as you go through it, it can also be a wonderful adventure. In my experience, as you make your way through, it gets much lighter, and, in the end, it's actually quite fun. Basically, hang in there if the beginning is rough. That would not be unusual, and it is definitely worth it.

The questions have been organized in the order I believe would be most useful for someone at the beginning of their journey of self-awareness into self-regulation to self-mastery and finally self-transcendence. They appear generally in the sequence they were helpful to me and the way that seemed to make the most intuitive sense.

Having said that, reading through all the questions and the stories around them will hopefully create a spark that helps you start, rekindle, or stoke your own fire by generating your own questions.

Finally, at the end of each question section, you will find a challenge/invitation—the "Your Turn" section—for how to use the question(s) in your own life so that you can experience, rather than just intellectually understand, the effect the questions can have. You can also utilize the "Your Turn" section proactively to train-in mental skills that will leave you better prepared for the inevitable twists and turns in this journey we call life.

There is a concept called the Four Stages of Learning (or sometimes the Four Stages of Competence). It is usually drawn as a circle, but I think it's more accurately a spiral. That spiral takes us from unconscious incompetence (where we don't even know what we don't know) to conscious incompetence (where we are painfully aware of what we don't know) to conscious competence (where we now know, but we have to think about it) to unconscious competence (where it's second nature and we don't even need to think about it anymore). And then we start the spiral again at the next level. This book is intended as a tool to help you navigate that spiral, no matter what part of it you are on.

My hope is that it will serve you well and assist you in the relentless pursuit of becoming "better," in creating the life you desire, and in serving others well. Godspeed.

1

Self-Awareness

Renowned author David Foster Wallace tells a story about two young fish who are greeted one morning by an older fish swimming by who says, "Morning, boys, how's the water?" The young fish swim on until eventually one says to the other, "What the hell is water?" Wallace's point is that water is so ubiquitous to the fish that they cease to be aware of it.

So it is with us. Our thought patterns, beliefs, values, and the stories we create about our lives have morphed in our unconscious or subconscious minds often since before memory. They are born out of the culture and circumstances we grew up in, and once they have been installed in us, they can become insidious, and it can be very difficult to become aware of them and root them out. Left unrecognized and unaddressed, they can wreak havoc in our lives because we are rendered unable to *re-spond* from a place of conscious choice. Instead, we *react* based on beliefs or thought patterns we're not even aware of. If we don't take the time and make the effort to learn what triggers our reactions, we don't have a prayer of creating the life we desire because we are constantly being thrashed around by our circumstances and our emotional reactions to them.

In order to change anything, and in order to construct the life we intend, we must first become aware of the "what is" in our lives and in our minds. It's difficult, if not impossible, to get from here to there if you don't know where "here" is. Or "there," for that matter.

The questions in this section are useful to begin the journey of self-awareness and self-discovery. These questions can help us become aware of the "water" in which we live—in other words, assist us in ferreting out unconscious limiting beliefs and unproductive emotional patterns.

They can also serve to create a space for movement after a period of feeling stuck because they help us recognize the stories we create and how we act in accordance with our understanding, perspective, and interpretation of those stories. Once we begin to use the questions to become aware of the stories, we can change them (since we're the author anyway) or we can get curious and begin asking more questions to discover the actual or more objective truth.

We can get ourselves in trouble when we concoct a story in our head about what somebody else's words, behavior or intention mean, especially when we are fabricating the story based exclusively on our perception and interpretation. Often, the very next thing that happens is that we react to that story without addressing its validity or, heaven forbid, clarifying it with the person we're making it up about, and, before you know it, an entire ugly downward spiral has begun. These questions can be instrumental in mitigating all of that.

In short, the questions in this section are designed to bring our unconscious patterns and beliefs into awareness so that we can consciously decide how we want to move forward. We are no longer subjected to the tyranny of reactivity. We are restored to the essential gift of our humanity—we are, once again, at choice.

?

- *What am I thinking/feeling?*
- *Is it true? Has it ever not been true?*
- *Does the story (still) serve me?*

These questions are particularly useful for cultivating awareness. They are great for beginning the journey of self-discovery or for getting unstuck. A good time to ask them is when you notice you're feeling something you'd rather not be feeling, thinking something you'd rather not be thinking, or when some aspect of your life is consistently not working.

The *What am I thinking/feeling?* question helps cut through the internal fog to figure out what the underlying cause of the upset is.

Once you have identified what the thought and the underlying feeling are, asking *Is that true?/Has it ever not been true?* will assist in identifying whether you've made up a story about it. It will create awareness that you are the one who has ascribed meaning to the precipitating event which is excellent news because that means you have the power to change it if you so choose.

I learned the *Is it true?* question from Byron Katie's four-part process called "The Work" that encourages people to end the self-induced suffering caused by their unrecognized beliefs.

Using *Is that true?* allows you to begin to determine whether the belief has any validity and whether you want to keep it, modify it, or discard it, or ask more questions.

4

If you decide that the belief actually **is** true (be careful not to fool yourself here), actively seek evidence to the contrary by following that question up with *Do I know every instance where this might or might not be true?"* These questions are very effective for deconstructing limiting beliefs and preventing reliance on dangerous assumptions and misperceptions.

Whether or not you determine that it is absolutely true, the last question *Does the story still serve me?* will direct you to examine your options and consciously choose your response.

I had an enlightening experience with this set of questions at a personal development workshop at the beautiful Miraval Resort in Tucson, Arizona. Master facilitator Wyatt Webb runs a program there called the Equine Experience. The workshop participants were taken from the resort to the equine facility where the workshop was held. We were seated on benches outside of a corral. Wyatt sat inside the corral on a stool not far from a horse tied to the corral rail.

Wyatt assigned us each the task of lifting the horse's hoof, cleaning it, and letting go of it. He demonstrated how to do it and then called us in, one by one, to attempt it ourselves. To provide context here, working with horses is particularly effective in demonstrating the concept of "how you do anything is how you do everything"—or at least how you do most things.

Just before it was my turn, the horse relieved himself and left a big pile of manure behind him. When Wyatt directed me to do so, I began walking toward the horse. Wyatt stopped me and asked what I was thinking. I said that I was nervous that the horse wouldn't lift his hoof

5

for me. Wyatt asked me what I thought that would mean. I said I thought it would mean that I wasn't internally clear or being congruent (because if you aren't, the horse won't). Wyatt told me to go ahead.

When I asked the horse for his front hoof, he gave it to me. Relieved, I cleaned it and set it down gently. "What was that about?" Wyatt asked me. I said, "What?" confused because I didn't know what he was asking. He said, "Do you always take the other's responsibility?" because I had set the horse's hoof down instead of letting him do it himself. Hmmmm. Something to think about.

Wyatt then nodded for me to proceed to the back hoof. I sidestepped the pile of manure and bent down to ask the horse for his hoof again when Wyatt said, "Hold it." I stopped, and he asked me if stepping around other people's "mess" (he used a different word) was a regular pattern for me. Hmmm. Something else to think about. Then he asked me what I could have done differently. I came up with several different options, but he kept asking, so I knew I wasn't getting to the answer he was looking for. In exasperation, I said "I'm not good at this thinking outside the box stuff." At which point, he said, "Really? Is that true?"

And so I was given the opportunity to think of times when that hadn't been true (contrary evidence) and to begin to 1) deconstruct that limiting belief, 2) be aware of when I was letting that pattern persist, and 3) choose a different story and a different response.

YOUR TURN

The next time you're feeling out of sorts, ask yourself what you're thinking that is causing you to feel that way. And then ask *Is it true?* If you think it is in fact true, consider times when it hasn't been true. Finally, ask yourself if it still serves you. If it does, great. You'll hold onto that then. If not, you can examine your best options and begin the process of choosing differently.

?

♦ *When is the first time I remember feeling this feeling?*

While this is similar to the first set of questions, this question is particularly good for becoming conscious of old ingrained patterns; for breaking through the oppression of reflexive, **unconscious** emotional reactions, commonly referred to as triggers; and most importantly for creating the space to choose differently in the present moment.

In my late 20s, when I began my personal development journey, I was about as unconscious as they come. I was working in the entertainment industry in what I would characterize as a highly dysfunctional company. I had dreamed of working in film or television production for years and had moved myself across the country to work in Hollywood. While I had heard the stories about what that might entail, I was completely unprepared for the craziness that had become a daily occurrence in that company.

Interestingly, despite the almost constant chaos, there was one woman who was consistently the eye of the storm. No matter how much insanity was going on, she always remained calm, collected, and self-possessed. Because I was growing weary and emotionally exhausted from the relentless drama, I became desperate to know her secret. So I decided to ask her how she was able to remain so composed.

She explained that she had grown up in a family where alcoholism was prevalent and she had attended Al-Anon for many years where she had learned a variety of tools for dealing with emotionally charged situations. So I started going with her.

Initially it was helpful, but I soon decided that Codependents Anonymous (CoDA) was probably a much better fit for me because it went right to the core of the emotional turmoil that caused many people to want to anesthetize with a substance—and made me want to dive into a quart of ice cream. My emotions were totally out of control and regularly flung me around and shook me up.

I went to a CoDA meeting, recognized it as perfect for me, and joined. Early on, a phenomenal sponsor helped me learn to navigate the muddy waters of emotional tumult. It was he who first taught me to use this question to discover unconscious emotional triggers that were adversely impacting my life.

He explained that whenever someone was having a reaction that was disproportionate to the current situation, it was likely because the current event was triggering an older, **unresolved** event (or pattern of events). He taught me to become aware of what it felt like to be triggered and, when I realized it was happening, to ask myself *When was the first time you remember feeling that feeling?*

At the time, one of the things that was a regular trigger for me was when somebody I was dating didn't follow through on something they said they were going to do. When this would happen, I would lash out, or even end the relationship, because I "wasn't going to put up with that!" (disproportionate reaction). After my sponsor taught me that tool, the next time it happened, I asked myself what I was feeling and when I first remembered feeling it. What came up was that I was feeling that person didn't value me, that I wasn't important enough for them to uphold their stated plan or intention. (It was too early in my development for me to have realized it likely had much more to do with them than me.) And the first time I remembered feeling not important, insufficient, or unworthy was when my parents divorced.

I also realized that there had been many times when I hadn't kept my word to myself, that I had let myself down, and I could see how that was being reflected back to me in other people's behavior. Those realizations about how I was feeling and when I first felt that feeling allowed me to separate out how much of the intensity of my feelings belonged to the current situation and how much belonged in the past.

Each time I worked with the question, I had the opportunity to look at what was actually happening in the present, what had happened in the past, and what meaning I had created around it. The benefit of this was that when I became aware of my triggers, I learned to differentiate between a reaction to the current situation and one that was exacerbated by accumulated, unresolved issues from the past.

The more I used that question, the more the feeling of being thrashed around by my emotions began to dissipate. And then I could begin to create enough space between the event that upset me and my reaction to ask myself questions that would either minimize or eradicate the effect of the triggering event.

It was a process that took a long period of hypervigilance and still takes refreshing from time to time, but it is worth every minute and every ounce of effort.

Your Turn

The next time you find yourself **disproportionately** upset about something that is happening in the moment, ask yourself the question: *When is the first time I remember feeling this feeling?* See what you can figure out from that. You might journal about what comes to you from that question the first few times you use it. That may allow you to see if patterns become apparent that will guide you a little deeper into awareness and reveal to you what needs to be healed or what steps you can take to keep from being triggered in the future.

Alternatively or in addition, you can train-in awareness proactively by simply remembering a time when you were reacting disproportionately to a situation, asking the relevant questions, and noticing any patterns.

?

• *What have I done to contribute to this feeling?*

This question follows in a logical progression. Like the previous question, it is also helpful when you're feeling disproportionately upset, but this one forces you to take *ownership* of the upset which puts you in a position to actually do something about it. It's a tough one because it's about owning what's yours and recognizing proper attribution, but it is ultimately extremely rewarding because it shifts you from being the victim and playing the blame game to being in the driver's seat of your own life. The catch is that first you have to take full personal responsibility—even when you believe it may not be your "fault." I found the best time to use this question is when you're feeling upset by something you *think* somebody else caused you to be upset about.

I remember the first time I was conscious enough to consider it. I'd been working with my CoDA sponsor for a while, and he had been asking me this question whenever I was upset and blaming somebody else for what I was feeling. This time, he wasn't around, but his training paid off because I heard his voice in my head and remembered to use the question myself.

It was Valentine's Day. I was in a relatively new relationship and very excited to shower my new Love with gifts, attention, affection, and quality time. I got off work early, stopped at the store to pick up flowers and balloons, prepared a lovely meal, set the table complete with candles, wrapped the gifts I'd purchased for him, signed the "perfect" card I'd found, showered, and got ready. He was a little late, but I shrugged that off and poured us each a glass of wine. We ate dinner, and then I began giving him his gifts. His lack of enthusiasm was a little disheartening, but I pressed on. Then, he gave me what he had bought for me—a rather generic card.

After he opened his gifts, instead of retiring to the bedroom to make love as I *expected* we would do, we watched television until he got tired and then went to bed where he promptly went to sleep. Probably needless to say (at least to many women reading this book), I was upset.

I was so agitated (i.e., triggered) that I couldn't sleep and got up and went into the living room. Then the question popped into my head. What did *I* do (or not do) or say (or not say) that contributed to what I was feeling?

The answer was that I thought/assumed/expected that he would respond to my overtures differently than he did. I had a plan in my head and a scenario all laid out, but when reality didn't comport with my vision—when he didn't respond the way I **expected** that he would or thought that he "should"—I became disappointed.

I had also made the mistake of investing in the relationship disproportionately to his investment—not a good idea. At that point, I had to own that the root cause of my disappointment was my own thought system. My expectations were both uncommunicated and likely unrealistic, and in many ways had set him and myself up to fail. Not to mention that I was attempting to control the entire situation and was not open to alternative outcomes. And, possibly worst of all, I "gave" with the expectation of receiving, which, of course, is no gift at all.

That recognition was the first step in learning to catch myself whenever I started trying to set up a situation to get another person to respond (or feel) a particular way. It was the first step in my learning to be aware of my expectations, communicate them when appropriate, and be open to different scenarios that could unfold—maybe better ones than I'd anticipated or planned. It was the beginning of my understanding that when you try to so carefully construct and control every minute detail, you leave no room for the spontaneous unfoldment of something potentially better. It also marked the beginning of my ability to monitor my emotional investment in a relationship relative to my partner's.

Finally, it was an opportunity to decide how to proceed going forward from that moment. I had the choice to continue to let my emotions control my attitude and my experience, or to own my contribution, take what I could from the situation, and move forward. I learned that, until you take responsibility for your life, you are powerless and at the mercy of other people and circumstances. But once you do take responsibility for your experience, you are empowered to change it.

YOUR TURN

The next time you find yourself disproportionately upset at a situation, ask yourself the question, *What have **I** done (or not done) or said (or not said) that is contributing to this feeling?* Once you realize what that was or is, you are then empowered to decide what you would like to do going forward.

You can proactively train-in this mental skill by re-membering an instance when you blamed or maybe are still blaming someone or something else for a "negative" emotion you had. You can then figure out what **your** con-tribution was to your own upset and decide how you want to proceed in the future.

?

- *What am I saying to myself?*
- *What is my self-talk?*

These questions can create awareness of your self-talk, help you tune into the tone and intensity of what you're saying to yourself, and give you space to elect to speak to yourself in a more affirming and productive way.

Here's my personal experience with this question. My ticket for Jack Canfield's weeklong Facilitating Skills seminar was gifted to me, so I decided that my contribution would be to play full out—to do whatever was asked of me and to maximize what I learned there to serve others to the best of my ability.

It was around the second day when we were given a homework assignment called The Mirror Exercise. The instructions were to look at your reflection in the mirror, say hello to yourself, and tell yourself all of the things you did that day that you were proud of. And you were to finish by saying, "Oh, and by the way... I love you" while you were looking into your own eyes.

Well, let me just tell you that I thought that was the most ridiculous thing **ever** and my first, very strong instinct was to say there was no way I was going to do it. But Jack and his facilitators knew that would be a common reaction, so after they described the homework assignment, they had a number of people get on stage and tell their stories of how much resistance they felt initially, but then how extensively the exercise transformed them and their lives. They basically communicated that it made them aware of the way they talked to themselves, that it wasn't pretty in the beginning, but as time went on, they became much more gentle and compassionate with themselves. Oh, and then there was that pesky commitment I'd made to myself to play full out, so I knew I had to do it.

When I got back to my room that night, I did. It was very difficult—it's amazing what it brings up—but I did it. It felt really disconcerting, but I was glad I'd kept my commitment. The next day we were assigned the exercise again—only this time we were supposed to do it naked. In addition, we were to thank our body parts for what they did for us. You can just imagine how well that went over in my head. I thought, "These people have lost their minds!" But I did it. And then the craziest thing happened.

The seminar was held at the University of California, Santa Barbara campus. We were staying in dorm rooms, genders segregated by floors. Each floor had a communal bathroom and shower facilities. On about the fourth day, I went to get ready before the seminar and realized I had forgotten a particular eye makeup pencil. And this is what I said to myself in my head, "You f^&$ing idiot! What the f^&$ is wrong with you? Is this a new campout for you?!"

Just a little harsh, right?! But this time, for the first time, I heard what I had just said to myself, and it stopped me dead in my tracks. I was horrified at the words, the tone, and the vehemence. For the most part, I wouldn't dream of speaking to another human being like that, but it was okay to talk to myself that way? The reality was that it was worse than just okay. It had become commonplace.

After that, whenever I caught myself talking to myself that way, I would stop and think of a way to communicate internally like I was somebody I cared about. And that was the beginning of a very big shift in my life because you can't fix what's broken if you're not aware that it's broken. And The Mirror Exercise is phenomenal for creating awareness of what we say to ourselves in our head.

This question can be immensely useful in another way. There is a ton of chatter about how depression is on the rise with young people because of all of the comparisons being done through social media. First, let me share the best thing I ever learned about comparison to others that has kept me pretty insulated from this affliction. A mentor I had in my early adult years said, "Comparing yourself to someone else never has a good outcome because either you feel you fall short, which makes you feel bad, or you feel superior, which isn't good either." I imagine most of us have heard the admonitions about not comparing ourselves to somebody else's "highlight reel" or not comparing somebody else's outsides to our insides. I've found it's hard enough comparing myself to former or envisioned future versions of myself!

A thoughtful and humorous concept on this subject comes from entrepreneur, life coach, and internet show host Marie Forleo who calls this practice "Compare-schläger" inspired by the nasty hangover people can experience from the aftereffects of too much "Gold-schläger," a Swiss cinnamon liqueur with visible flakes of gold in it. The questions *What am I saying to myself?* and *What is my self-talk?* can be a good safeguard against a Compare-schläger hangover!

Last, but certainly not least, these questions offer an important reminder to start speaking to yourself in a supportive way. High performance and sports psychologist Dr. Michael Gervais says that confidence comes only from credible self-talk. So it's super important to start speaking to yourself in ways that acknowledge, affirm, and uplift.

YOUR TURN

It may very possibly feel odd. You may very possibly hate it. But I guarantee that, if you choose to do The Mirror Exercise every night for 30 days (which is what we were assigned), you will become keenly aware of the way you talk to yourself. That awareness will allow you to change your self-dialogue so you can stop keeping yourself down and instead lift and encourage yourself into the next better phase of your life. I really can't recommend it highly enough.

You might also keep these questions in mind any time you're spending time on social media platforms that tempt you to compare yourself with others. Notice what you're saying in your head and see if it's something you care to change or stop.

There are certainly other ways to become aware of your self-talk (meditation, for example), and, if you prefer to try one of those, great. But I strongly suggest you do the work to cultivate self-awareness of what's going on in your head because, without it, it's highly unlikely you'll see any changes for the better.

?

- *What story am I telling myself?*
- *What am I making it mean?*
- *How can I imagine this better?*

These questions are invaluable for creating the understanding that we are the authors of the stories of our lives. As such, we get to determine, create, and interpret the stories the way we choose. Of course, we don't get to determine all of the situations and circumstances of our lives, but we 100 percent control how we view them and what we make them mean. So these questions help us see if the stories we're currently telling ourselves are working for us and, if not, how we might want to change them.

This was a tremendously provocative question for me in my mid-50s. I'd gone back to the Miraval Resort for a life-coaching-through-horses intensive program, again with Wyatt Webb. During one of the processes, I was complaining about feeling stuck in my life. Wyatt asked me where I was feeling stuck—in what area of my life. I told him it was about my career versus my calling and explained the "situation" (i.e., told him my story and excuses). He then asked me how long I'd known that the job I was in wasn't where I felt I was supposed to be. My own answer floored me. "Decades."

I'd worked in law offices on and off for most of my life, even though I always knew I should be doing something in the personal development space. I would take brief hiatuses from the legal field to try something different, but I'd always go back because the money was better.

I thoroughly related to Michael Corleone's quote from Godfather Part III: "Just when I thought I was out, they pull me back in!"

But as miserably unhappy as I was for long periods of my administrative career, I never took the steps necessary to move from there into what I believed I was meant to do and what my soul longed for. Why? Because of the story I told myself. I told myself that I had to endure the misery of working in a cubicle because I needed the security of a full-time, nine-to-five, regular-paycheck job in order to pay my bills and feed my four-legged kids. Master life strategist Tony Robbins talks about divorcing your story when you discover that the one you've been telling yourself isn't serving you. It was time to divorce my story and ask the next question *How can I imagine this better?* to create a new, more empowered, more compassionate, and more productive story. One where I no longer continued to wallow in misery and play small.

I rewrote the earlier version of my story to something more like this: "That may have been true once, but the reality is you're like a bamboo plant that spends years growing its root system before it ever sprouts, but, once it does, it just takes off! You've spent decades accumulating the life experience and wisdom you need. Now it's time to share your gifts with the people around you **while** you're devising, strategizing, and implementing your exit plan. Then you can share what you've learned on a bigger scale and in a much larger arena, starting, for example, with a book about self-discovery and useful questions."

Much better story.

YOUR TURN

These are good questions for when you feel stuck or dissatisfied with something in your life. If either of those is true for you, figure out the story you're telling yourself (for example, the excuses you're making or the "reasons" for the situation). A good way to facilitate this line of questioning is to imagine that someone asked you about why you're stuck or dissatisfied and why you don't change it and then listen to your own answers.

Once you've figured out the story, reconsider it and decide how to craft a better story for yourself—one that validates, uplifts, and empowers you.

?

- *What does it matter?*
- *Will it matter five years from now?*
- *Will it matter when they're dead?*

These represent the question equivalents of the statement, "This too shall pass." I have found them extremely helpful in two different ways.

The first is to calm myself down when I'm in an argument or at a standstill with someone who is important to me. The questions provide a perspective on really just how important the argument is in the grand scheme of things, especially in comparison to how important the person is to me. They also allow me to let go and move forward instead of holding onto something and letting it fester.

My stepmother had a lovely British friend who would say, "What does it matter?" I thought that was such an endearing way to make a very important point. And there's a similarly wonderful quote from M.C. Escher who said, "If it doesn't matter in five years, it doesn't matter."

I try a similar approach when I find myself in that awful place—an argument or a stalemate with somebody who is important in my life. I think about how I would feel if this was still unresolved when they died. More than anything else, this forces me to realize that the relationship is more important than making my point.

I had a very close friend die when I was in my mid-30s. His name was Dave Seret. He was 45 years old, successful, in great shape, and very precious to me. He dropped dead from cardiac arrest after a day of skiing in Colorado with our ski club. I wasn't on that particular trip, and I was beyond stunned when a mutual friend told me what had happened.

Before his death, we talked at least daily, sharing the everyday details of each other's lives. Though there was never anything physical or romantic between us, we were very clear on how we felt about each other—we loved each other dearly. In the days and months after his passing, I came to realize what a monumental gift it was to have known that with such clarity and certainty. At the time of his death, there was nothing unsaid between us, nothing unresolved, nothing to regret. Somehow, that made the loss of him a little bit easier to bear.

It was a profound lesson that I have taken with me into every day since. It reminds me how fleeting life is and how we can be here one minute and gone quite literally the next. **That** helps me appreciate moments with the people I love on a very different level. It also makes it a whole lot easier to let the small stuff go—and often even the not-so-small stuff. For me, that question *Will this matter when they're dead?* really cuts to the center of what really matters.

YOUR TURN

Is there somebody in your life that you are currently at odds with, in an argument with, or possibly no longer speaking to? If so, it's a good time for these questions.

If that's not the case at the moment, but you find yourself in an argument or at a standstill with a loved one or a cherished friend at some point in the future, stop to ask yourself these questions. Will what you're arguing about matter in five years? What about when they're dead? What if they died with this unresolved? How would that affect you? How might it affect your children or anyone else the relationship touches? How important is it **really**?

Hopefully, these questions will make you consider what's truly important and permit you to let go of the need to be right or to hold onto a problem at the expense of the relationship with an important person in your life. Time is short. None of us is promised tomorrow. *What does it matter?*

?

♦ *Then what?*

This is such an insightful question to really determine whether you're on the right path or if your ladder is on the wrong wall. Like the previous questions, it helps you anticipate the likely consequences of your actions several steps down the line.

One of my all-time favorite illustrations of the power of this question is the parable of an investment banker who goes to a little fishing village to try to convince a fisherman to scale up his business. Here's the story, as recounted in Erin Loechner's book *Chasing Slow* (paraphrased):

An investment banker was at the pier of a small coastal fishing village when a small boat with just one fisherman docked. Inside the boat were several large fin tuna. The investment banker complimented the fisherman on the quality of his fish and asked how long it took to catch them. The fisherman replied, "Only a little while." The investment banker then asked why he didn't stay out longer and catch more fish. The fisherman said he had enough to support his family's immediate needs. The investment banker then asked, "But what do you do with the rest of your time?" The fisherman said, "I sleep late, fish a little, play with my children, take a nap with my wife, stroll into the village each evening where I sip wine and play guitar with my friends. I have a full and busy life."

The investment banker scoffed. "I am a Harvard MBA and could help you. You should spend more time fishing and with the proceeds buy a bigger boat, and with the proceeds from the bigger boat you could buy several boats. Eventually, you would have a fleet of fishing boats. Instead of selling your catch to a middleman, you would sell directly to the processor, eventually opening your own cannery. You would control the product, processing, and distribution. You would be able to leave this small coastal fishing village and move the big city, where you will run your expanding enterprise."

The fisherman asked, "But how long will this take?"

To which the investment banker replied, "Fifteen to twenty years."

"But then what?" asked the fisherman. The investment banker laughed and said, "That's the best part. When the time is right, you would announce an IPO and sell your company stock to the public and become very rich; you would make millions."

"Millions?" asked the fisherman. "Then what?"

The investment banker said, "Then you would retire. Move to a small coastal fishing village where you would sleep late, fish a little, play with your kids, take naps with your wife, stroll to the village in the evening, sip wine, and play guitar with your friends!"

Then what? is also an intuitive question for learning to regulate your own behavior and begin to develop self-mastery. In his book, *The Daniel Plan*, Pastor Rick Warren discusses using this question to assist with health goals. He writes, "*Then what?* The two most powerful words, when it comes to your health, are ***then what***. These two small words can literally change your health in a positive way if you keep them at the top of your mind. If I do this, *then what* will happen? If I eat this, *then what* will happen?... Think about the consequences of your behavior before you act."

Another amazing application of this question comes from Native American culture. They have an ancient philosophy stating that decisions they make today should result in benefits for seven generations into the future. I can't actually conceptualize that myself, but in my view it's an incredible way to develop foresight. I imagine it is extremely powerful in developing a sense of personal responsibility for the decisions you make and the consequences of those decisions for yourself and those after you.

This idea has had a big impact on helping me stay motivated to share what I have discovered so far. As I progress in my life and share what I've learned, I hope it will accelerate the learning and perhaps shorten the suffering of someone who comes after me. I like to imagine that maybe someday, possibly long after I myself am dead, maybe seven generations down the line, something I learned and shared might be useful in someone else's journey.

Ultimately, the *Then what?* question can be used very effectively in order to imagine the consequences of **any** behavior. Examination of potential consequences is extremely revealing to create choice points that lead to intentional responses.

If I just take this one drink, *then what?*

If I let my emotions get out of control and start behaving in a hostile manner, *then what?*

If I set my mind to achieving a particular goal, *then what?*

If I love with my whole heart, *then what?*

Then what? A powerful question.

YOUR TURN

The next time you find yourself deliberating about what action to take or at some other choice point, ask yourself *Then what?* and keep asking the question until you feel satisfied that the direction of your choice is the right one for you and anyone or anything you care about. It can be a tremendously useful guide, and it just might prevent you from having to endure unintended and undesirable consequences.

?

- *What is this REALLY about?*

This question is very applicable for going deeper into your own psyche to get underneath the surface chaos to the heart of the problem so it can be cleared up, fixed, or healed.

When I first took my one-year-old horse, Fame, to the Parelli Natural Horsemanship school in Pagosa Springs, Colorado, the teaching staff had posted a phrase on the chalk board that said, "It's not about the…" That was to remind us that if we couldn't get our horse to do a particular task, it wasn't about that task or the obstacle. It was **really** about something else.

Many people weren't able to easily get their horses into a trailer, so the instructors would say "It's not about the trailer." I was having absolutely no success at getting my baby horse to step over a six-inch-wide "creek." I remember being very frustrated because I knew "it wasn't about the creek," but I didn't know what it was **really** about. I tried what I thought was **everything** to get that boy to step over the tiny stream of water—cajoling, begging, threatening, bribing, but he was having none of it. As I was going through all my machinations, an instructor came by. She could see my frustration and asked me if I could just accept that I was right where I was supposed to be. That smug question was just the icing on the cake at that moment, so I told her I thought maybe I should be done for the day, and she agreed that was a good idea.

The next morning, when all of the students gathered into our *remudas* (herds) to do our classroom work, I asked about what was **really** going on there. It turns out that with horses (as with many people) agreement or refusal isn't about the object (trailer, creek, etc.). It's about whether sufficient trust and respect exist between you. I'd let my horse get away with murder for the better part of a year, and, as a result, he had absolutely no respect for me. In my ignorance, I'd also asked him to do things during that year that hadn't worked out well, so he didn't have a lot of trust in me either.

This question is so important because if you don't ferret out what's really going on, you just go around and around in circles dealing with the symptom instead of the root of the problem. Once I understood what the **real** issue was, I was able to work with the horse in ways that built respect and trust. Before we left, he was hopping over the "creek" like nobody's business.

Another place I find this question particularly useful is with secondary emotions. In my youth, due to a number of irregular circumstances, I learned to process uncomfortable emotions by converting them to anger. But the anger was secondary to the initial emotion which was usually hurt or disappointment. For me, the anger was easier. It felt more powerful than to sit in the rawness of vulnerability. But the problem was that when I reacted with anger, nothing got resolved. Nothing got better. And in many cases, the situation got much worse. The person I was trying to communicate with would get emotionally flooded and couldn't hear me. It wasn't until I could stop and ask myself the question *What is this **really** about?* that I could shift back into the initial emotion and begin

31

to communicate from an authentic place that gave me a much better shot at being heard and the possibility of finding an amicable resolution.

YOUR TURN

The next time you are experiencing an intense negative emotion like rage, anger, or frustration, or whenever a recurring pattern brings up an intense negative emotion (like a recurring fight between life partners), stop for a moment and take some time to analyze *What is this really about?* Dig deeper into what lies underneath the surface. Look for the patterns and what they reveal to you. Consider what feelings preceded the intense negative one because they are allowing you this opportunity for insight. If you don't take the time now, you're just putting a Band-Aid on a gaping, festering wound that is highly unlikely to heal on its own.

Of course, if you want to be proactive, think about a time when intense negative emotions were up for you, or ways you know they come up for you, and then peek under the Band-Aid to see what's **really** going on there.

?

+ *What are my emotions trying to tell me?*

This question can be life altering. It can take you from feeling at the mercy of your emotions to seeing your emotions as guides, tools, and signposts. And that is a cataclysmic shift in perspective.

Instead of trying to suppress negative emotions by pouring a drink, lighting up, popping a pill, or scarfing up bonbons, this question helps us analyze our emotions so we can discern what they are trying to tell us and what we are being asked to understand or do. Instead of just waiting for them to pass, going to war with them, or being overrun by them, we can actually use them to move us from self-awareness to self-regulation.

I remember a time when I felt completely trampled by emotions on a regular basis. It was very disruptive in my life. The tail was definitively wagging the dog. It was then I was introduced to the idea of emotions being signposts and call-to-action alerts (Tony Robbins again). As I started to work with this question, I realized how useful it was for stopping unpleasant, uncomfortable, or even painful emotions from running roughshod over me and, more importantly, for beginning to transition to the next level of personal evolution.

When we can keep a more open mind, remain curious, even investigative, it keeps us from trying to run away from emotional discomfort which is hugely important; growth cannot occur when we're eschewing negative emotions. A line from a Robert Frost poem comes to mind: "the best way out is through." That's sure been true for me.

At a granular, tactical level, here's my personal experience with using my emotions as signposts. I have a bit of shame about this story, but I'll tell it anyway because I think it's illustrative.

I moved from Michigan to California when I was 28 years old. I had been living in Los Angeles for a couple of years, and I was unaware (obviously, as you'll see) how much stress I was under, how easily agitated I had become, and how low my tolerance had become for pretty much anything even mildly annoying.

During that time, my mom and stepdad decided they wanted to retire in California, and they made a trip out from Michigan to see if they could find a retirement residence. They found a condo they liked, and they asked my sister and me to take off work the next day to come down to Carlsbad to see it. If we liked it, they were planning to buy it and rent it out until they could retire and move out to California.

The realtor showed us the condo, which we loved, and then asked us all to lunch in the charming small village center. We parked across the street from the restaurant, and, as I was crossing the street (and jaywalking by the way), a woman driving her car in my direction honked her horn. I immediately and reflexively lunged toward her car and screamed, "What's your problem, lady?!" while aggressively throwing my hands up in complete frustration. It turned out she was a friend of the realtor's and was honking to say "hello." Not my proudest moment.

But I decided to use it as an opportunity to see my emotions as signposts. Why was I so easily agitated? Why was my frustration threshold almost nonexistent? Why did I fly off the handle at **nothing**? What were my emotions of frustration, anger, and hostility trying to tell me?

They were trying to tell me that I'd been burning the candle at both ends—and from the middle—and had completely neglected self-care. I had allowed my emotional immune system to become completely depleted. The result was that even the slightest stressor (or even imagined stressor) was enough to set off a maelstrom. I still refer back to that lesson to this day. Whenever I find myself being short-tempered or easily irritated, I know immediately to check my self-care. Almost without exception, it's been neglected whenever those emotions are present.

It was an incredibly enlightening experience that continues to serve me well—all from the question *What are my emotions trying to tell me?*

Your Turn

Regard any intense, pervasive or negative emotion in your life as a signpost. Ask it what it wants you to know. Figure out what it is trying to get you to see. Is there something in your perspective that needs to change? Or your behavior? Is there a relationship issue you need to address? Is there some pillar of self-care you've been neglecting? If you dig deep enough, you will likely find the answer. If you're stuck, keep trying different things until the emotion dissipates. That's when you'll know you have figured out a message underneath the emotion.

2

Self-Regulation

Once self-awareness has become a regular occurrence, the next step is to shift our focus from external circumstances, situations, events, and other people to internal references and conscious intentions.

The questions in the previous section helped us gain awareness of our triggers, limiting beliefs, and hidden patterns so that we could expand our choice points enough to be able to consciously respond versus merely reacting. The questions in this section will assist in **directing** our choices at those choice points. We will begin to make conscious choices about what those responses will be and how we want to conduct ourselves in the daily business of living. The questions guide us to discern between what is or is not in our control, and they put us in the driver's seat over our own thoughts and actions.

These questions also remind us of possibilities and potentialities, and they gently prod us to keep our focus. They aid in directing the trajectory of where we want to go, how we want to get there, and who we want to be along the way.

?

- *Who/how do I want to be today?*
- *How can I best conduct myself in this relationship/ situation so that I will be proud of myself?*

These questions can be applied in several ways. First, they are extremely effective in eradicating victim mentality, they empower you to gain control over strong emotions in difficult situations, and they assist in purposefully creating the best version of yourself. They are instrumental in formulating an intention of how you want to show up in your life every day. Once you set that intention, it greatly increases the likelihood that you will have that experience.

I remember actually typing out the first question and taping it up on my bookshelf where I would see it every day when I was several years into what had become a very difficult marriage.

I had allowed my marriage to deteriorate to the point where I was in a state of near constant misery. I didn't know how to do it better and didn't know where to go for help. I also didn't want to give up, and the frustration created by those conflicting emotions was intolerable. In my desperation, I was angry, bitter, hostile, and hopeless. I'd have to say it was definitely the proverbial dark night of the soul. I had become completely reactive and felt absolutely at the mercy of my emotions.

And then I came upon that question *Who do I want to be today?* Irrespective of the fact that my husband has fallen prey to alcohol and prescription drug addiction to a degree that I hardly recognize him, *Who do I want to be today?* Irrespective of the fact that I have been living in a construction zone posing as a house for three years with concrete floors, stud walls, and no kitchen sink, *Who do I want to be today?* Irrespective of the fact that I go to work every day and come home to nothing having been accomplished and then have to shift gears to work on the house for several hours at night, day after day after day, *Who do I want to be today?*

This was HUGE in getting me to stop playing victim (something I thought I'd never do, but was now my normal MO). I had become so accustomed to blaming my husband and his choices for my feelings and the situation I found myself in that I had completely lost my sense of self and the power I had over the sovereignty of my state. And I knew better.

So I kept asking the question *Who do I want to be today?* Sometimes I had to chunk it down to the smallest increment available to me *Who do I want to be in this moment? How do I want to react to what is happening right now?*

That led to *How can I conduct myself in this relationship/situation so that I will be proud of myself?* And that was the beginning of the road back to the reclamation of my soul.

In the end, those questions were responsible for creating beauty from ashes in helping me reconstruct a better version of myself out of the shell I had allowed myself to become during that time.

YOUR TURN

These questions can be considered every day and sometimes multiple times a day. *Who do you want to be today? What is your intention for how you want to show up today? How do you want to conduct yourself generally? And in connection to specific situations or people? How do you need to conduct yourself so that you will be proud of how you showed up at the end of the day?* Or more importantly, at the end of your life.

?

- *What is the source of my worth?*
- *What is the source of my identity?*
- *What am I basing my self-esteem on?*

This is an important set of questions because they go straight to the core of who we are/who we think we are. Since everything we do flows from that, it makes sense to give them some serious consideration and treat them with respect by taking the time and giving them the attention they deserve.

In addition to being useful for defining the source of your worth and identity, they are also helpful when you have been overidentifying with a particular **false** source of self-esteem. If that source is no longer available to you or you recognize that your growth requires you to let go of it or transcend it, these questions can bring clarity. Examples could be an executive who derived his identity from his position and/or net worth who finds himself unemployed after a merger or downsizing or a woman who derived her sense of self-worth from her physical attributes who is now aging.

Finding the answers to these questions can be very empowering because, in the end, they always lead back to the **true** source of your worth, and the true source can never be diminished. The task then becomes to re-identify with *that* source instead of the false point of identification previously embraced. Finally, these questions allow us to give ourselves a choice about what to intentionally build our self-esteem on.

Dr. Christopher Mruk, a professor at Bowling Green State University, has a revealing matrix that illustrates the components of self-esteem.

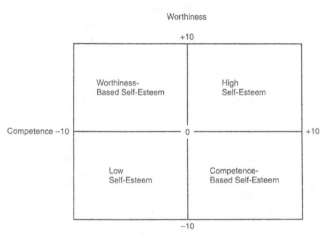

Source: Modified from Mruk, C. J. (2018, 2013)

Basically, self-esteem is derived from how competent we think we are, combined with how much worth or value we believe we have. Competence is about your abilities at doing something—sports, your job, creating something, etc. It has to do with the skills and experiences you've acquired. Worthiness is your internal feeling about the value you have as a human being.

I remember when I first discovered his theory because I finally understood myself so much more clearly. From the time I was a small child, I was extremely confident in my own capabilities. My parents tell a story about taking me to a new church for the first time and how I didn't even wait for them, I just opened the door and went right into my Sunday school class completely unfazed. I had been taught that there was nothing I couldn't do if I set my mind to it, and I believed it.

So I didn't really understand why, as an adult, I kept allowing people into my life who didn't treat me well and why I continued to make choices that were an obvious attempt at self-sabotage. When I saw Professor Mruk's model, it all made sense. I knew that I had confused competence with self-esteem. And I knew then that I was in the quadrant of high competence/low worth which then made me analyze why I had such low self-worth. The question *What is the source of my worth?* clarified external circumstances in my youth that were in play.

Because these things had occurred from early childhood, I had adopted other people's ideas of my worth by osmosis before I ever gave it a conscious thought (as is the case with many self-destructive patterns). From a very young age, I was regularly noticed and acknowledged for my physical appearance. I never realized that became the thing that I based the "worth" part of my self-esteem on. I had so over-identified with it, and it was such an integral part of who I was, that I had never even considered whether my appearance was what I wanted to base my worth on. The belief was installed in me long before I was ever aware of it.

Not long after being introduced to the Mruk model, I attended *A Course in Miracles* lecture by author-spiritual teacher, Marianne Williamson. At that time, when you came into the theater to hear her speak, you were given "miracle cards"—small cards a little larger than a business card that contained quotes from the book, *A*

Course in Miracles. The one I got said, "Your worth is not established by _____ [*Fill in the blank*]. Your worth is established by God." I still have that card because it started the shift from linking my worth with something external to the understanding that our worth is inherent.

Many years later, I was listening to an *Impact Theory* podcast by founder/host, Tom Bilyeu. He talked about **choosing** what you base your self-esteem on and how that had helped him shift from a fixed to a growth mind-set. It occurred to me that even though your worth is inherent, if you later attach your self-esteem to something that you have no control over (consciously or otherwise), it will have significant influence on how much or little you value yourself. A good way to ensure a high sense of personal value is to combine the belief in your inherent worth with the attachment of your identity to something valuable that is within your control. For Tom, that combination was that humans are the ultimate adaptation machine and that he could learn anything.

While it is vitally important to base your self-esteem on what **you** decide it should be based on, it is also critical that it's based on something within your control—something that can't be taken from you. For me, one of the gifts of aging is the recognition that basing my self-esteem on my appearance is not, and never was, a good idea. So I combine the belief in my Creator-established worth with the choice to identify with and feed my self-esteem by how I conduct myself and, in particular, how I contribute to other people's lives.

When you choose to base your self-esteem on something within your control—whether that is a be-lief or an action or both—something that can never be taken from you and something that you value, **even if it is something you don't currently have or do**, you set yourself up to succeed.

YOUR TURN

These questions really warrant taking some time to think about because they are the very foundation from which so many of our thoughts, beliefs, and actions stem.

Ask yourself what you are basing your value on. What is it that you identify with? Is it your intellect? Your financials? Your appearance? Your ability to make somebody else laugh? Then decide whether what you are currently basing your self-worth on and what you identify with is enriching your life or depleting it. Was it something you consciously chose, or did it happen under the radar? Is the source of your self-esteem something within your control? Do you want to adhere to whatever has been the source, or choose a new one? And last, but most importantly, I'd invite you to adopt the belief that your worth was established by your Creator (whoever or whatever you believe that is). That belief is something that can never be taken away from you, and it is a great place to start.

?

- *What's the worst case scenario?*
- *How would I handle that?*
- *Given this, what's the best option?*

As usual, these questions are useful in several ways. Let's start with dealing with fear. I love some of the definitions I've seen for the acronym F.E.A.R.: False Evidence Appearing Real, F^&$ Everything and RUN (but that's not us!!!), and my favorite, Face Everything and Rise.

One area where these questions are very effective is in fighting fear. Public speaking is a huge source of fear for many people, so let's take that as an example. If you have to make a public speech and that has you feeling anywhere from anxious to terrified, you could ask yourself *What's the worst case scenario?* Perhaps you forget what you're going to say, or the equipment for your PowerPoint presentation doesn't work, you lose your notes, or you vomit or faint. Now ask yourself *How would I handle that?*

You might take a minute to collect yourself, maybe even explain that you are nervous and continue; you could ask for assistance in getting the equipment running or do without the PowerPoint; you could talk from your experience, or better yet, from your heart; you could clean yourself up, get up, and move on with your day and your life **or**, if you're in the "advanced class," you can figure out how to use whatever showed up for your benefit or the benefit of others.

Remember that we **construct** stories that may not (and in most cases probably will not) come to fruition. As

Mark Twain said, "I've lived through some terrible things in my life, some of which actually happened."

If you catch yourself making up a negative story about the future (that is, worrying or feeling anxious), or even if you have consciously chosen to use the worst case scenario exercise, be sure to follow it up with the best case scenario. Intentionally make up a good story about the outcome. In the case of the public speech, maybe it's that you are really happy with your delivery, that your audience loved you, your boss or the people that hired you complimented you, and you get a promotion or are hired to do more speeches. Master life strategist Tony Robbins says, "If you're going to make up a story anyway, why not make it a good one?"

A word of caution about the worst case scenario method: The mind is very powerful in causing what we vividly imagine—in thoughts and imagined experiences—to come to fruition. The subconscious mind is especially good at creating what we picture in our minds and feel or react to in our bodies.

In 1988, the book, *You Can't Afford the Luxury of a Negative Thought*, was released. The title was particularly true from a brain chemistry perspective. Here's a layman's explanation of how our brain works: When we think new thoughts, we create new neural connections in the brain. When we think recurring thoughts, we strengthen those connections. Imagine the first thought as a trench. The depth of the initial trench will depend on your emotional state at the time. Then imagine the recurring thoughts as deepening the trench. After a prolonged period of thinking the same thought, installing beliefs, telling ourselves the same story over and over again, the trench can begin to look like the Grand Canyon. So we would be well advised to be aware of our recurring and/or emotionally charged thoughts and do our damnedest to make sure they're positive because it becomes increasingly difficult to take a new turn of thought when you're thousands of feet (metaphorically) down the canyon walls.

All of which is to say, try to spend as little time as necessary on the worst case scenario, and with as little emotional charge as possible. Try to imagine it from a detached place as though you're watching a black and white movie.

Conversely, spend the bulk of your time really digging into the meat of the best case scenario. Imagine it in full color as if you're right in the middle of it actually happening. Imagine what it looks, sounds, smells, tastes, and, most importantly, *feels* like. Get excited because that emotion is the fuel for the vision. Heavy-hitting entrepreneur and host of the *Impact Theory* and *Health Theory* podcasts Tom Bilyeu recommends the 80/20 rule here—spending 20 percent of your time on imagining the worst case scenario as motivation to get going and 80 percent on imagining the best case scenario to envision what you want to create.

Both Marie Forleo, mega-successful entrepreneur, life coach, speaker, and internet show host, and performance expert Todd Herman recommend a similar technique that they call "scripting your setbacks" (although I think a more appropriate description would be "scripting your comebacks"). It's an insightful tool for mentally rehearsing what your response will be when you experience a setback or a negative reaction or criticism.

My understanding is that you start by thinking about, or better yet, writing out the description of a situation you have been ineffective at changing or that you are dreading. You then think or write about how you want to conduct yourself differently in the future—what that would be like—and the choices you want to make the next time the situation presents itself. Remember the more powerfully you can enroll all of your senses in experiencing the positive change, the better the shot you have at having it come to fruition and the faster it will become manifest.

That's how those questions can be used in dealing with fear and motivation. They can also be instrumental in allowing us to get around limiting factors that we see as "realities."

I had a personal experience using these questions to accept what was "true" at a particular time without becoming resigned to it. The questions became a great launching pad to create a new reality by shifting to a solution orientation instead of staying stuck in the problem.

I was working as a secretarial coordinator in a mid-size law firm in West Los Angeles. My boss, the director of human resources, had a very uncompromising and authoritarian management style which was difficult for the assistants as well as for me.

When I would hold team-building meetings, they often began with a deluge of complaints about this man. While I felt the same way, it would not have been appropriate or productive for me to chime in, but, if I ignored the comments, I risked alienating my team by minimizing or failing to consider their feelings. So, I first acknowledged that "it is what it is at the moment" by stating the current reality (that it didn't appear he was going anywhere anytime soon). I then asked the question that redirected the prevailing train of thought, the question that created a U-turn if you will, the question that pulled the discussion from a narrow dark path out into the open where light could be shed on new possibilities. That question was this: *Given this* (the fact that they worked under a very difficult manager who would likely be around for some time), *what are our best options?* This question refocused the discussion on the solution rather than the problem.

A way to expand on that is to personalize the situation—to ask how can I best set myself up for success **within the given parameters**? Again, there is an acknowledgment of the starting place—of the "what-it-is-ness" of the moment—but the question itself stimulates movement away from that current reality and more importantly *toward* what you are intentionally creating.

Your Turn

The next time you start to worry or feel anxious or afraid about something (or if you want to train for this, recall a time when you felt any of those feelings), **briefly** consider the worst case scenario. Remember to think of it from an emotionally detached place. Picture it as though you're looking at a black-and-white photograph. Don't spend more than 20 percent of the time you have for this exercise thinking about the worst case.

Next, think of the best case scenario, or an outcome you would like to see come to fruition. Really sink into the vision of this until you can see it in living color and you actually experience what it would/will be like when that is happening. What do you see? Smell? Is there a taste? What do you feel on your skin and in your heart? Spend at least 80 percent of the total time you have imagining this best case scenario.

And last but not least, ask yourself, *Given this, what's my best option?* or *Given this, how can I best set myself up to succeed?*

?

- *What can I do?*
- *What else could it be/mean?*

These questions can be deployed for several purposes—to help us see possibilities, to break through tunnel vision, to encourage us to think outside the box, to expand our perspective, to change our mindset, and to dissipate worry—all of which give us a feeling of empowerment and create a solid sense of self-efficacy.

When I first heard this question put to use, it stunned me because I wasn't really aware that the natural tendency for many people is to focus on, or at least give more attention to, the things we CAN'T do, or are "prevented from" doing. That was made abundantly clear in an equine-assisted learning session I was co-facilitating. In those sessions, there are at least four participants: a licensed mental health practitioner, a horse professional (me in this case), a horse, and the client or clients. The sessions typically take place inside a closed corral or arena. The therapist and horse professional create a task for the clients, go through a short safety briefing, explain the goal of the task, possibly give certain parameters, and then sit back and observe what transpires as the session unfolds. After a period of time or when the clients feel they have completed the task, everybody comes back together to process what happened within the session.

The task for this group was to get a horse to move from point A to B, without breaking the following rules: 1) no talking, 2) no touching the horse, and 3) no use of anything outside the arena to assist in accomplishing the task. The clients tried asking a lot of questions about what they were or weren't allowed to do, and the therapist simply reiterated the three rules she had stated initially because that's part of the process.

Realizing they weren't going to get their questions answered, the clients went about their task. When it was over and the post-session processing was underway, much of their focus was on how difficult it was in light of the restrictions that had been placed on the situation. It became very apparent that everyone was much more focused on what they COULDN'T do rather than exploring the innumerable options that *were* available to them—what they COULD do.

The therapist brought that to their attention and then extrapolated from the lesson, asking them how often that happens in their everyday lives—how often are we so concerned with or consumed by what we can't, shouldn't, or aren't supposed to do, that we completely miss or lose sight of what is available to us or possible? And what effect does that have on, not only our lives, but the lives of everyone we touch as well? The craziest thing about that session was that there were only three restrictions, three CAN'Ts, if you will—but there were **countless** possibilities, countless CANs, that they just weren't seeing.

A few years after that session, I was working in a law office with an office administrator who was very into sharing self-development techniques with the staff. One day he called me into a conference room and asked me if I wanted to play a personal development game. Being the self-improvement junkie I am, I said, "Of course!" He asked me to pick any object in the room, so

I picked a drinking glass. He put it on the table in front of us and asked, "What is it?" I said, "A drinking glass." Then he asked the magic question *What else could it be?* I said, "I guess it could be a vase." He asked again, "What else could it be?" I said, "A paper weight." He then asked me to try to come up with 10 other things it could be in one minute.

The exercise was very effective (and much tougher than I expected it to be). It showed very clearly how easily we can get locked into a certain mindset about what things are or mean. More importantly, it showed me how to break out of that mindset—to think outside the proverbial box. When I extrapolated from that lesson, the "box" represented my own perspective which has been created, shaped, and molded by multiple influences including genetics, culture, epoch, etc.

I started using the *What else could it be?* question and have found it very helpful in a variety of settings, but particularly in combatting worry. It's also very effective in counteracting the concoction of negative stories we make up, and it's wonderful for expanding a current situation, vision, or dream.

My sister and brother-in-law have an amazing marriage steeped in deep trust that has been more than earned over many years. We always joke with her saying he could come home drunk, reeking of perfume, with lipstick on his collar, and my sister would say, "How sweet is he?! He was probably out trying new wines to find one I like, testing perfumes to buy me a new one, and having a salesperson show him different colors of lipstick for me and then used his shirt to clean off his hand." Of course this is over the top, but you get the point. That would be a very extreme (and possibly unwise) utilization of the *What else could it be?* question.

That question can also be an effective tool to keep yourself from misinterpreting communication. If you find yourself taking offense at something someone said, ask yourself *What else could it mean?* Maybe the word they used doesn't have the same meaning or connotation to them. *What else could it mean?* Maybe the comment wasn't directed at you. *What else could it mean?* Maybe the person was having a horrible day, and they hadn't had enough sleep and didn't handle the situation as well as they might have. *What else could it mean?*

This is hugely relevant in today's world of electronic "communication." Instead of thinking that somebody didn't respond to your text because they're upset with you, or they're not interested in you, ask *What else could it mean?* Maybe they're just busy! *What else could it mean?* Maybe your message never got to them. *What else could it mean?* Maybe they're figuring out how they want to respond.

The point is, these questions open us up and make us aware of other options. They show us new ways to look at things and offer us an array of other perspectives. We are then empowered to **decide** to choose what best serves us.

And the best thing about this tool is that the more you use it, the more automatic it becomes and the more options you are able to see.

YOUR TURN

The next time you're feeling stuck, instead of focusing on what you can't do, or what you've already tried that didn't work, ask yourself the question *What CAN I do?* and keep asking it until you come up with a different focus and new strategies so you can see and step in a different direction.

The next time you start to worry or make a negative assumption, ask yourself *What else could it be?* or *What else could it mean?* Come up with as many answers to those questions as you can and then **choose** one positive option to ruminate on. Better yet, realize that there are any number of things it could mean and **decide** to distract yourself and move on until the facts or the truth reveal themselves.

If you want to do more advanced work to expand your perspective or ward off worry, **recall** times you felt stuck, times you worried, or times when you assumed the worst about something. Ask *What could I have done?* and *What else could it have been/meant?* Consider what the outcome *actually* was and recall that memory to reassure yourself the next time you're tempted to fall into that trap.

The bottom line here is to use *What else could it be/ mean?* to disable worry, fear, or other negative fabrications. Play the game of *What else could it be?* and see how many **positive** alternatives you can come up with.

?

- *What do I choose to focus on?*
- *What's good about this?*

These questions can prevent you from getting into a funk, help you get or stay out of emotional darkness, train yourself to look for the good, and source your life with joy.

The first time I used these questions successfully was a pivotal moment. I had invested a lot of time listening to Tony Robbins' content on the power of focus just before a vacation I took to Costa Rica with my mother. We were staying at a beautiful resort on the ground floor right on the Pacific Ocean. A few days into a fantastic trip, as we were getting ready for bed, my mom asked if I minded if she left the sliding glass door open, and just closed the screen, so we could hear the ocean. I never locked my doors, so I thought it sounded like a lovely idea. Around three in the morning, she woke me to ask if I had just come through the screen door. I said, "No," and starting feeling around on the nightstand for my iPhone which I was using as an alarm clock because we had an excursion the next morning. The phone wasn't there. I got up, turned on the light, and discovered that thieves had broken into the room **while we slept**. In addition to my phone, they stole our rental car keys, my wallet, and some of my mother's travel jewelry.

We called hotel security who called the Costa Rican police, we filled out a police report which was no small feat since neither of us spoke Spanish, and the police ostensibly didn't speak English. Then we called the rental car company who initially said they would need to send a second set of keys from San Jose and that would take several days (by which time we were supposed to be back in the States).

After all the commotion died down and we'd done everything we could do, I went for a run on the beach. Initially I was a bit shaken up, but as I ran down the beach, those questions ran through my mind. Here was the proverbial rubber meeting the road. This was the gist of my internal dialogue: "Well, Corrinn, *what are you going to* **choose** *to focus on?* And *what's good about this situation?* You can focus on the bad—the fact that you just got robbed and that, because your rental car keys were stolen, you're going to miss the excursion you had scheduled. You can be mad that it happened and that your phone and all of your vacation pictures are gone. You can be mad at the resort and/or the police, and you can fabricate stories about setups and the treatment of American tourists in foreign countries—all of which will leave you in a highly agitated, emotional state. **OR,** you can focus on the incomparable beauty of this beach and all that's good here, in this moment. You can focus on the fact that you're healthy and strong enough to be able to run on this amazing beach; that neither you nor your mother was hurt; that your passports were safely locked in the safe so you will be able to fly home in two days; that the rental car company brought another car to the hotel and the excursion let you reschedule; that your mom still has her phone and plenty of vacation photos on it; and that you still have two more days and many more things to do and see in this glorious place."

When I got back to the room, I was in a great frame of mind, and my mom and I were able to fully enjoy the rest of our trip. It was such an incredible experience to see how the simple act of choosing and directing my focus quickly and significantly impacted my state of being and the quality of my life in that moment. That experience was the perfect embodiment of this wonderful quote from Russell M. Nelson, "The joy we feel has little to do with the circumstances of our lives and everything to do with the focus of our lives."

YOUR TURN

The next time you're feeling out of sorts or down, examine what your thoughts have been focused on. Sometimes it helps to identify those thoughts, but it's not necessary—often the awareness of feeling "off" is enough. Then ask yourself, *What do I choose to focus on now? And what's good about this present situation?* The second question can be more difficult, but there is almost always good to be found if you pursue it hard enough.

As always, if you'd like to do more advanced work, you don't have to wait until you're feeling out of sorts to use these questions. Make them a part of your routine so that you become increasingly conscious of and intentional about what you want to focus on and you train yourself to seek the good.

?

♦   *What can I do to nourish my body/mind/spirit today?*

I have used this question to recover from being depleted, as well as to keep from getting depleted.

Before I learned to nourish myself on a regular basis, I allowed myself to get into serious physical, psychological, and spiritual deficits. A dear friend gave me a lovely book called *The Art of Extreme Self-Care* by Cheryl Richardson. After reading it, I decided to make a list of the things that leave me feeling replenished and restored. I set out on a conscious practice of picking something (or a few things) from the list and doing them when I was in a low spot. It had the wonderful effect of helping me realize that **staying** nourished is key. So I began implementing these actions on a regular basis and particularly when I felt susceptible to fatigue or irritation.

Here are a few items from my list:

- Being around a large body of water
- Taking in a movie
- Puppy time
- Getting a massage
- Taking a hike/spending time in nature
- Laying hands on my horses
- Holding an infant
- Immersing myself in beauty
- Immersing myself in gratitude
- Undertaking regular physical exercise (5 times per week)

- Working daily meditation and better nutritional choices into my regime (still working on this one!)
- Enjoying a daily practice of listening to, watching, or spending time with people that are intentionally or naturally positive.

Motivational speaker Jim Rohn famously said that you are the average of the five people you spend the most time with. I realized that most of the people I was spending my time with were less positive than I was, so I starting spending enormous amounts of time reading positive books, listening to positive podcasts, seeking out coaches/coaching advice, looking through the filters of professional athletes or holistically successful people who possessed the common thread of irrepressible positivity.

In recent years, I've come to call this soul nourishment practice "feeding the good wolf." It comes from a popular legend, sometimes attributed to the Cherokee. An old man is teaching his grandson about internal conflicts in his life. He tells the child that a terrible fight is going on inside him between two wolves. One is evil—anger, envy, sorrow, regret, greed, arrogance, self-pity, guilt, resentment, inferiority, lies, false pride, superiority, and ego. The other is good—joy, peace, love, hope, serenity, humility, kindness, benevolence, empathy, generosity, truth, compassion, and faith. The grandfather explains that the same fight is going on inside the grandson—and inside every other person too. The grandson thought about it for a bit and then asked, "Grandfather? Which wolf will win?" The old man simply replied, "The one you feed."

After hearing this story, I had a major revelation. It occurred to me that "bad wolf food" is ridiculously prevalent (at least in our society today) and that I needed to take extra care to feed the good wolf or she wouldn't have the strength to keep the bad wolf at bay.

The really important part of this was that I realized I had to feed my good wolf **in sufficient quality and quantity and with sufficient consistency** to counteract the food the bad wolf was getting. Instead of just a routine regular practice, I noticed the importance of counterbalancing the amount of bad wolf food coming in. If the bad wolf was getting the normal amount of food, then a normal level of good wolf food was enough. But if the bad wolf was getting extra food (i.e., life was extra challenging for a time), then my typical way of feeding my good wolf wasn't going to be sufficient. I had to ratchet up her care to meet the increased demand being placed on her and I had to be hypervigilant about when she needed an increase.

What that means literally is that I needed to take note when I was feeling depleted, agitated, easily frustrated, or just off. And when that was the case, I had to do something **extra** to nourish my soul and take better care of myself **in direct proportion** to the degree of "off" I was feeling.

I don't always notice when my good wolf is hungry, but I'm getting much better at preventing it, noticing the signs of neglect, and responding more quickly now.

YOUR TURN

First, you have to figure out what your good wolf likes to eat because it's different for everybody. In other words, consider what nourishes your soul and refreshes your body. I'd strongly recommend making an actual list of those things. The next time you're feeling out of sorts, overwhelmed, depleted, irritable, or just a bit off, go to your list and do as many as needed to right yourself.

The advanced work here is to consistently and proactively nourish and care for your body and soul. Frequently check in to see if your self-care is at the level it needs to be, given the current circumstances of your life, your body, and your mind.

?

◆ *What can I be grateful for right now?*

I cannot overstate the importance of this question for an exponentially enhanced experience of life. There is nothing I've learned that is more powerful.

Here's the story of when I first identified this question and began to use it.

The weeks leading up to my birthday that year had been filled with joy and love, but on the actual day I felt as if the universe had conspired against me. By the end of the day, I was feeling pretty beaten up. On my drive home, as I often did, I called my best friend who I call my shamanesse. I regressed into old patterns of complaining, "venting," and generally telling (okay, retelling) stories that didn't serve me. Worse than that, they were stories that fed the bad wolf. And then I told her how upset I was with myself since I knew that I knew better.

In her wisdom, she asked me what it was that I knew I should be doing. I told her I should be shifting my thoughts to the things in my life that I am grateful for right now. Again, in her wisdom, she simply asked **this** useful question, "Would you like to do that now?" See how brilliant she is?!

And so I began. Normally, gratitude is an exceedingly easy exercise for me, but I noticed that in the state and mindset I'd worked myself into, it was considerably more difficult than usual. It felt like the flow was constricted. So I went back to what I knew would always get me started—a process I'd named "being grateful for the NOTs."

I'd discovered this process years before when I was working in another law firm. I hadn't yet figured out that my mental state and the story I told myself were largely within my control so I was blaming my daily misery on the fact that I was working in a career that was sucking my spirit dry. It was such a dark point in my life. I felt completely incapable of elevating myself out of the cesspool I'd made of my life.

At that time, I was reading an excellent book by Viktor Frankl called *Man's Search for Meaning*. Frankl was a holocaust survivor who had noticed, while he was in the camps, that some of the prisoners withered and perished quite quickly, but others survived and still others were able to actually thrive, even in that hellacious environment. In the end, he concluded that the difference was whether the person had meaning in their life and a sense purpose (or at least held onto the idea of a future meaning and purpose).

While this was an important discovery, his graphic and horrific description of life in the camps was even more significant for me at that time. It caused me to think, "Well, at least I'm NOT in a death camp," and "I'm NOT forced to work with a gun to my head," and "I'm NOT doing hard labor in the freezing cold with tattered clothing and shoes with holes in them," and "I'm NOT going to work every day with a human incinerator looming over me while I wonder if today is my turn." This is the process I now refer to as being grateful for the NOTs. And that process created just enough of a crack for a sliver of light to get through. That light illuminated some of my blessings and, more importantly, started a snowball effect, shifting my perspective to recognize how many things I could be grateful for right now, like "I have my freedom" and "I'm incredibly healthy" and "I have a decent job that pays me enough to provide a nice life for myself" and on and on.

Today, I spend 5 to 10 minutes every morning on gratitude, and I never run out of things to be grateful for. I find it beneficial to group them in different categories, for example, gratitude for relationships, past and present; something that is present in my life, or something I'm glad is NOT in my life at the present time; and/or one "small" thing (like clean drinking water, paved roads, or a flower in my path).

The biggest category for me is to express gratitude for different parts and systems in my body. I start with my sense of sight and consider deeply what an incredible gift it is and how it is not one that is afforded to everybody and how it should be cherished—revered even. And then I start to go through all of the lovely things in this world that I am able to take in through that sense: my adorable Yorkies; my powerful, regal horses; our family lake house; the epic vistas of my ranch; the beautiful faces of my nieces and nephews; and **colors**! And then I start to think about all of the things I take in through my sense of sight by color—the spectacular blue sky with crisp, white puffy clouds, the deep red of an American Beauty rose, the intense fuchsia of the stunning bougainvillea bushes... And then I'm off into the things I take in through my sense of sight in nature—the incomparable palm trees of southern California, the gorgeous beaches here. And on and on.

Interestingly and unexpectedly, whether I'm being grateful for my eyes and everything I take in through them (which alone could take a lifetime to appreciate), my hearing, my sense of touch, my strong legs that carry me wherever I want to go, or my heart and circulatory system that pump and clean the blood that courses through my veins, this process is really helping me improve my relationship with my body.

One magical "side benefit" to the practice of gratitude is that it's self-reinforcing. Various psychological studies indicate that feelings of gratitude produce feel-good chemicals—"reward" neurotransmitters in your brain—the same ones that are produced in addicts when they're getting or even anticipating a fix—so the more you practice gratitude, the better it feels and the more you want to do it. How's that for a fabulous win-win?!

The other great "side benefit" is something called priming. Priming means "to prepare something for use or action," like when you prime a pump before using it. When you experience gratitude, you prime yourself to notice more things to be grateful for, which is why I particularly love to do this practice in the morning. It sets you up to notice more things to be grateful for all day—**even** in the presence of things to the contrary.

My sister plays a sweet game with this every day. She calls it "looking for the trinkets." She believes that God has placed little gifts for her throughout her day, so each day becomes a treasure hunt, and she is primed to find lovely surprises during her whole day. What a marvelous way to go through life.

Your Turn

This question works best to keep you in a good state of mind if it's practiced every day. But it can also be useful to shift you to a more positive mindset if you're going through a dark time or you're just feeling a bit down.

Ask the question and then open your eyes to see everything that is present (or absent) that you can be grateful for. My mother has a sign on her refrigerator that says, "What if you woke up today with only the things you were grateful for yesterday?"

You can take advantage of any of the tools here—being grateful for the NOTs, for the parts and systems of your body, for your relationships, for anything present in your life, and "small things." Of course, you can always develop different categories or methods of your own to find the goodness in your life.

I'd also invite you to incorporate priming into your life. Set yourself up to be geared for finding and seeing the unlimited number of things to be grateful for. Search for the trinkets.

This is really a guaranteed key to a better experience of life.

?

- *What now?*
- *What's next?*

These questions target areas where we may be stuck. Sometimes, even if we have a vision, we're clear on our dreams, we know where we are and where we ultimately want to be, we can feel stuck because either we're overwhelmed by all there is to do to effectuate those dreams and create the vision, or maybe we just don't know the steps, the how. Sometimes we want to see the whole map in every detail before beginning the trip. What tends to happen in any of those scenarios is the state of internal paralysis, i.e. feeling stuck.

The most useful tool I found for dealing with this came from Jack Canfield's segment in the movie, *The Secret*. It became such an important metaphor in my life. Until that point, I would paralyze myself with over planning and perfectionism. I had a hard time starting a project or pursuing a goal until I had every single step mapped out in minute detail which, of course, never happened.

In the segment, Jack utilizes a metaphor of driving at night. He says that if you are going to drive from California to New York, it's not important that you see the entire route—only that you see the next 200 feet ahead of you. At that point your headlights will light up the next 200 feet, and your route will keep unfolding before you. He says trusting that each 200 feet will become visible will allow you to get eventually to your destination.

So it is with our goals, visions, and plans. It's important to consider the potential consequences of our actions and choices to make sure our ladder is on the right wall—that we're starting off on the right path—but once we have determined that our direction is right, we just need to see the next step or two to get started. Then we use the feedback we get from taking that step to determine the next. And so it goes. Two hundred feet at a time.

YOUR TURN

Whenever you're feeling stuck, after considering the potential consequences of whatever choice you're faced with, you can use this question to get you out of analysis paralysis and into action. All you need to do is determine the next step or two, take those steps, and then look at the feedback you got before taking the next one.

And, worst case scenario, if you can't decide between options for the next step, just pick one, do it and reflect on the result. You will almost always have the opportunity to make another new choice.

3

Self-Mastery

After self-awareness—becoming aware of our internal dialogue, thoughts, beliefs, and emotions—comes self-regulation—the ability to monitor and control our external responses. The eventual refinement of self-regulation is self-mastery, and I believe it is a lifelong process. It is also not likely to be a linear process. You will certainly make progress, sometimes quickly, sometimes more slowly; then there will likely also be times you'll regress and remember that you knew better.

But self-mastery is about continuing on a path of progression toward your best self. It is about the desire and intention to relentlessly pursue becoming better. It's about working toward automatically responding the way we would like to—as if it had become second nature. At times it can be frustrating. At times it can be discouraging. But most of the time, and ultimately, it is extremely rewarding. It leads to feelings of self-actualization and self-efficacy. It leads to living life in a place where you are who you authentically want to be. It leads to feeling empowered to navigate in the world while feeling complete congruence with who you are. It leads to living up to your potential. The following are the questions that help me the most on this perpetual quest.

?

- *What makes my heart zing?*
- *What/who inspires me?*

These questions are really about the experience, development, and harnessing of passion. The experience of passion in and of itself is a phenomenally life-enhancing one, but learning to develop it and harness it to move closer to who you want to be and what you want to create increases that experience by orders of magnitude.

In my life, it's been easiest to take action toward who I want to become and to create an intentional life when I am inspired and passionate. The three things I find most helpful in creating this experience are music, observing or being in the presence of mastery, and being out in nature in a particularly beautiful setting.

Music is so amazingly powerful in changing and creating moods and internal states. If I listen to music that is calm and serene (think Enya), I can literally feel my parasympathetic nervous system kick in and I start to relax. By the same token, if I want to energize myself to get into a workout, I will listen to hip-hop or some rap. If I want to enjoy my time with my horses on the ranch even more, I'll play a little country. And if I want to get inspired to get down to the work I believe I was put here to do, nothing does it for me like The Score or some Imagine Dragons. The point is, the varieties and complexities of music can really help change or induce a mood, soothe a battle-weary spirit, AND create a feeling of inspiration and passion. And that is a very useful tool.

Something else that makes my heart zing and never ceases to inspire me is to be in the presence of or witnessing a master at work. It is an enormously powerful and moving experience.

One of the most memorable times this happened was soon after the end of my marriage which was followed closely by the death of my stepfather whom I dearly loved. I was completely bereft and had absolutely nothing left. I was totally checked out of life and was just going to keep my head down, do the bare minimum to get by, and wait to die.

Then I found out that Chris Cox, a renowned master horseman, was coming to my town to give a clinic at our local riding club. I had revered this man for many years, and the excitement I felt about him doing this clinic at our club breathed new life into me. I desperately wanted to ride in the clinic, but I didn't have the money to buy a spot. Oh, and my horse was lame.

Strangely, little miracles started to happen. I was a member of the club's board, and, because we were hosting the event, the board was given one free ticket. We decided we would raffle the ticket once the clinic was otherwise full, but whoever won the raffle would have to pay full price that night. The raffle was to be held at our regular monthly potluck dinner, and I was dreading watching somebody else get the ticket—the last chance to ride in the clinic. The night came, the president of the club explained the conditions of the raffle, and incredibly, no one at the dinner entered the raffle. This was inconceivable to me except that I understood too well that most of us couldn't afford the ticket. I went to the president immediately and asked her if I could have it. I explained that I couldn't pay for it that night, but I would be able to in a couple of weeks which was before the clinic was to start. She quickly called a quorum of board members together, and I was granted the ticket! Now I just needed a rideable horse.

At the time, my sister and a friend of hers were taking dressage lessons near my house at a considerable distance from their homes. They would come down once a week, do a lesson, spend the night, and go back the next day for another lesson. When I told them about the clinic, my sister's friend offered to let me borrow her beautiful horse Soleil.

Participating in that clinic was definitely one of the high points of my life. Witnessing Chris do what he was put on this earth to do was magnificent. I watched in awe as he repeatedly won the trust of these incredible prey animals within minutes. I felt the horses almost melt in relief at being handled by a master. The communication between Chris and each horse was immediate and seamless. It was truly a thing of beauty. And then there was the way he worked with each rider to help them become a better horseman and a better human being. By the end of the clinic, I was floating. It created a tremendous breakthrough in my life that led almost immediately to me dropping 30 pounds of weight without even trying, obtaining my coaching certification, and starting my company. Amazing what inspiration can do.

Currently, the mastery that inspires me each and every week comes in the form of two podcasts. The first is a podcast I discovered through Tony Robbins when he was interviewed by the über-successful entrepreneur Tom Bilyeu. Tom was one of the co-founders of a company called Quest Nutrition, and, as part of creating a healthy lifestyle, he began the *Inside Quest* podcast on which he interviewed thought leaders in a variety of fields. The mission of the podcast was to move people TO ACTION and to break them out of "The Matrix." Since I first found Tom and *Impact Theory*, he and his powerhouse wife, Lisa, have started a new company called "Impact Theory" and have changed the podcast name to the same, and every week, the information the guests share is both inspirational and extremely useful. But it is Tom's laser focus, relentless drive, and uncompromising commitment to excellence—his mastery—that keep me moved to action.

The second inspirational podcast is called *Finding Mastery* (which I found when its host Dr. Michael Gervais was a guest on the *Impact Theory* podcast). Dr. Mike is a sport and performance psychologist, and the co-founder of a phenomenal company called Compete to Create, and on his "pod," he interviews people who are pursuing mastery and/or have achieved it—most often, it's both. It is perpetually inspiring to listen to the stories of these men and women, what makes up their psychological frameworks, what they have been through in life, and what they have sacrificed to get where they are. But what is at least as, if not more, inspirational is witnessing the genius that is Dr. Michael Gervais—the way he mines, examines, and polishes all of the gems his guests offer up. The skill and finesse with which he frames his questions is like an invitation to dance. And dance they do. I wait with anticipation every week for the incredible gift he and each of his guests unwrap together. And the treasure he unveils each week is a tremendous blessing in my life that keeps me on track in my own pursuit of mastery.

Last, but certainly not least, is the mastery of the Creator evidenced by the indescribable natural beauty on this planet. Whether it's the majesty of a mountain range, the grandeur of a spectacular canyon, the simultaneous power and tranquility of an ocean beach, or "just" the pure and simple beauty of a wildflower, nature has always been and will always be a true source of inspiration for me. It will forever make my heart zing.

YOUR TURN

My invitation to you is to figure out what inspires you. And, more importantly, what inspires you to the point of taking action. Start to notice when you feel most alive. What is happening in those moments? Is it a location, a performance, a personal success or achievement? And what makes you feel so inspired or driven that you actually take action toward the realization of your **own** dreams or life goals?

Once you have discerned what those things are, find a way to bring more of them into your life. Find a way to utilize the energy they give you and use them to begin (or continue) to create the life of your intention. That all starts by asking *What makes my heart zing?* and *What/who inspires me?*

?

- *What kind of life do I want to create for myself?*
- *What would I ultimately like to see?*

These are profound questions about creation. Questions about possibilities. Questions about expansion. And at the same time, questions about clarity. They can be asked with respect to any situation. I've found these questions particularly important to set the trajectory of my life and to keep me on an upward spiral of personal development and next level living.

Obviously, they are big, overarching questions, so I tend to revisit them once or twice a year and then focus on the daily objectives that move me in the direction set by the questions. What's been most helpful to me in goal setting, once again, is to break them down into several categories. Usually at the beginning of each calendar year and again around my birthday, I think about what I would like to see come to fruition in the next year. Basically, I set my intentions for that next year in the following areas:

Physical: including health/well-being, finances, career, and my material environment

Mental: primarily mindset training (mindfulness practice, and training in thought patterns, habit loops, etc.) and what I would like to learn

Emotional/social: covering relationships and how I want to feel and express my emotions

Spiritual: this is about how I fit in the world, my relationship with/to the Earth and my Creator and how to spend more time being present with both and nurturing those relationships

Once I have the overall ideas in each of those categories established for what I'd like to see during the next year, it's much easier to set about creating a life that reflects those intentions. They represent the rudder of the ship. Without them, I would tend to drift out to sea for extended periods of time. Drifting now and then works for me, but I'm not a big fan of perpetual flailing, which is why I love these questions.

A lot of people have trouble with this. They seem to be looking for some grand passion or purpose that will determine the direction of the rest of their life. Sometimes that happens, but more often, passions and purposes are temporal and change in the different chapters of our lives, just as we do.

The best advice I ever heard on how to develop your passion or purpose came from, again, Tom Bilyeu. To paraphrase, he suggests paying attention to what *gets* your attention. Pay attention to what excites you—what lights you up. Follow that for a while, and it will either fizzle or spark.

I'd like to add that even if it sparks, or there is some recognition that "this is my purpose," it doesn't mean that will be true for a lifetime. Some people have lifetime purposes and passions, but it seems for most of us, those change during different periods of our lives. While I have a *lifetime* passion for learning, I have a *current* purpose of being there for my mom in her later years and a *future* purpose of building a ranch for girls who have survived sex trafficking. It's okay to have multiple passions and purposes during our lives. It's okay to pursue different avenues. It's okay to not have a singular, overarching purpose. Really. It's okay. You can still ask yourself what kind of life you'd like to create. And if you want to, you can change your mind.

That's also true for the *What do I want to create for myself?* and *What would I ultimately like to see?* questions in general. What I've realized about those questions is that the answers changed throughout my life. In my 20s, it was about the acquisition of material things. In my 30s, successful relationships became more important. In my 40s, it started to become about self-mastery (which will certainly take the rest of my life), and now, in my 50s, it shifts between all of those things at different times and in different measure, but it is also largely about sharing what I've learned and trying to add value to others' lives. It's about the active expression of deep and abiding gratitude. It is the reason I felt compelled to write this book.

The key is to think about what you'd like to see, but leave room for the possibility of something better.

YOUR TURN

My suggestion here is for you to avail yourself of these questions to discern what kind of life you intend and set a direction for how to create that. What do you want to do, have, experience, learn, and most importantly be? How do you want to show up in the world? What impact do you want to have? How do you hope you're remembered?

If you're struggling with discovering your passion and/or purpose, remember it's more about development than discovery. Just pursue what interests you, notice what captures your attention, and what takes your breath away. That's usually a good lead to follow.

?

• *How can I best set myself up for success today?*

Morning routines and/or night-before routines are a hot topic these days, and it's no wonder. They seem to be one of those "magic secrets" to high performance or even just doing what you're meant to do. They prime you to set yourself up for success each day.

I recently had the privilege of taking an incredible online course called "Finding Your Best" that I highly recommend to anyone interested in that topic. The course is replete with wisdom that facilitates personal success and fulfillment. I learned this short, powerful, four-step, morning ritual from the co-creator of that course, Dr. Michael Gervais, who is also the host of the *Finding Mastery* podcast.

Step 1 is to take a long, slow deep breath immediately after waking.

Step 2 is to call to mind something you're grateful for and recall the experience of that something.

Step 3 is to set an intention for how you want to be in the world that day.

Step 4 is to put your feet on the floor to ground that intention in.

It might look like this for me: wake up and take my deep inhale, feel the gratitude I have to be waking up sandwiched between my two adorable Yorkies, decide that the quality I want to embody today is being present, and put my feet on the ground to solidify that intention.

This is such a powerful ritual because it anchors you to your intentions from the first moments of the morning. You start your day by thinking about and declaring who and how you want to be. Another way to accomplish this is to plan your schedule, goals and intentions the night before. This has the added benefit of letting all that seep into your brain while you sleep. Imagine if you did that and then ran through a refresher in the morning!

The personal development world is replete with information on goal setting, so I won't regurgitate that here, except to say that my view is that deciding how you want to show up in the world while you are working on your goals is as at least as important as the goals themselves. It might be the difference between achieving a goal and feeling empty versus achieving the goal and feeling thrilled, proud, and deeply satisfied.

For example, to say you want to complete a kitchen renovation with your spouse is very different from saying you want to complete a DIY kitchen renovation with your spouse while remaining patient and loving and expressing encouragement and gratitude along the way. Similarly, saying you want to meet a targeted sales goal for the month is very different from saying you want to meet that goal while inspiring and lifting up your team and helping each individual team member move closer to the realization of their potential. It can be more difficult to include the qualities with which you want to achieve the goals, but the victories can be rather hollow without that step.

Another way we can set ourselves up for success is to recognize what we want to move toward and what we want to move away from.

Life strategist Tony Robbins addresses this in his material, and identifying those positions can be very powerful in teaching us how to harness our focus and power. It seems to be a natural inclination for humans to focus on what we want to move away from or avoid. To focus on what we don't want. To focus on the negative. We say, "I want to lose 30 pounds" rather than "I want to get to my optimal weight of ___ pounds." We say, "I don't want to fight anymore" instead of "I want to learn to cultivate our best possible relationship." I said, for years, "I don't want to be stuck in a job that sucks my spirit out of my body" instead of "I want to learn the skills and develop the mindset required to make a prosperous living by providing the most value, making the biggest contribution, and being aligned with my life purpose."

Perhaps more importantly, at least in my own experience, moving away from something (which is generally based on fear) usually takes Herculean effort and willpower, both of which are hard to sustain when the whole goal is to move away from the stimulus. Conversely, moving **toward** a stimulus or goal is more aligned with desire, intention, and passion. So it is generally a much more pleasurable and sustainable strategy.

Master neuro-linguistic programming practitioner, Dr. Topher Morrison, told a revealing story about this in a lecture I attended. He was demonstrating the difference between using will and imagination to achieve a goal. He said that he would set his alarm for very early in the morning to get up to go to the gym. When the alarm went off and he was laying in his toasty, comfy bed, and it was cold outside of the covers and still dark, if he tried to get out of bed by sheer force of will, overcoming all those obstacles in addition to inertia was very difficult. But he noticed that if he used his imagination in a specific way, it wasn't a problem at all. Here's what he did. He lay there and imagined what he and his life would look and feel like if he chose to stay in bed day after day foregoing his workouts. That was highly distasteful for him (something he wanted to move away from). Then, he would imagine what he and his life would look and feel like if he got up every day and completed his workout (something he wanted to move toward). Using his imagination to extrapolate from that one day to different likely outcomes in the future made getting out of bed to head out for the gym infinitely easier.

YOUR TURN

Here's the invitation for this set of questions. Find a morning or night-before routine that will prime you for success. Think about what your goal or intention is, what you want to accomplish, what you intend to create, and how you want to show up in the world and in your life while you're doing that. Then create a ritual you do every night before bed, or every morning when you wake up (or—hey—even both!), that supports the achievement of those goals and intentions.

As you move through each day, pay attention to what you're naturally inclined to move away from and toward and see how you can capitalize on that to realize your objectives rather than trying to strong-arm everything with sheer willpower. Envision how moving away from your desired state or outcome would play out and then use your imagination to experience how moving toward it would feel. The combination should serve you well.

?

- *What have I been successful at before that might help here?*
- *Who has done this (or something like this, or a part of this) before?*

These questions can be utilized to quell self-doubt and to increase certainty and confidence in yourself. They can also provide insight into more refined mastery, of your craft or your mind.

It's significantly easier to stay the course through times of self-doubt when you have a record of your past successes to RE-mind yourself (put yourself back into your right mind) that you have already acquired and possess many skills. You can also RE-mind yourself that you possess the qualities of character needed to acquire more skills and knowledge—qualities such as intelligence, creativity, grit, humor, etc.

When I took Jack Canfield's "Facilitating Skills" seminar, he had us do an exercise where we quickly listed as many things we could recall that we had been successful in for each decade of life. The gist of it is that you make a list of all of the things you've succeeded at from the time you were born. While it was tough to do, it was well worth it because it turned out to be a really effective tool for those times when I experienced self-doubt. During those times, it was difficult to recall when I had succeeded at something. Reviewing the list was liberating and very empowering.

Over the years, I added another element to it: I now list all those who facilitated those achievements in addition to the effort I contributed. Adding that part helps me remember those that have helped me along my path, and it helps keep me humble and grateful.

I actually made a table that has the success in one column and the people who contributed to that success in the next. Here's a small part of my chart:

Success	Contributors
Learned to walk	God, mom, dad
Acquired the English language	God, mom, dad
Learned to read and write	God, mom, dad, Ms. Smith (my kindergarten teacher)
Got PADI (scuba diving) certified	God, mom, dad, Jim Simmerman (my then boyfriend), JC (the divemaster)
Took women's 3rd in the 2003 World Hydrofoil Championships	God, mom, dad, Mike Murphy (inventor of the hydrofoil), the Century City Ski Club, my ex-husband who introduced me to it, Mike Mack, Trevor Sudweeks, Dani Martin, John Clemmons, Sandy Bertha (great riders)

Put everything down that comes to mind, no matter how small a feat it might seem. My chart starts with "learned to walk." In some ways, it seems like such a small thing, but when you spend just a few seconds thinking about it—what would life be like if you hadn't acquired that skill? Including it serves as a reminder to be grateful that I can walk! (If you can't, it can serve as a reminder to be grateful for the other things you **CAN** do.)

Another important takeaway from learning to walk is to recognize how many times you had to fall down before you mastered the skill of walking. Which means you started out in this life with tenacity. You started out with grit. You started out with perseverance. And you never saw **any** of the falls as a failure. You **instinctively** learned what worked and didn't work and incorporated it into the next try. Now consider the result and what the net value of that has been. What if you had quit? As entrepreneur Tom Bilyeu eloquently says, "The failures **are** the lessons!" Or as radio personality Bobby Bones succinctly reminds us, "Fail until you don't."

An expansion of this exercise is to reevaluate areas of your life that would typically be called a failure (though I prefer to regard it as feedback) and analyze the lessons you learned and the character strengths you developed by navigating those waters.

For example, my second marriage was a very difficult decade in my life, but I developed a resilience like no other as a result. And I learned to pay attention to and be grateful for the smallest good. It carved out deep compassion in me. That experience also taught me to begin to know when it's time to choose a different road. Those are valuable skills that I can use to build confidence and extrapolate to other situations in my life.

The legendary athlete, David Goggins (the "toughest man alive"), keeps what he calls a cookie jar which is where he has recorded the things in life where he initially "failed," but later succeeded at that very thing, or turned that loss into a huge win in another area of his life.

I loved this idea, so I decided to make my own cookie jar and to color-code the successes by category (physical trials I overcame, relationship issues I worked out, skills I learned, etc.). I put colored pieces of paper describing my own inspirational experiences in an actual cookie jar. Now, if I'm ever struggling with learning something new or overcoming some adversity, I can pull a piece of paper of the appropriate color from the jar and look at an example where I triumphed over something similar in the past. It's great self-therapy.

Both the success log and the cookie jar are reminders of what is possible from your own personal history. Another approach when you're struggling with something new is to resist reinventing the wheel by asking *Who else has done this (or something like this, or a part of this) before?* question.

This question keeps you from making the same mistakes others have made and usually significantly accelerates your own learning. As Tony Robbins is renowned for saying, "Success leaves clues." And I love the John Maxwell quote, "it's said that a wise person learns from his mistakes. A wiser one learns from others' mistakes. But the wisest person of all learns from others' successes."

This question capitalizes on mentorship and learning from both the "failures" and successes of others. It's about building on an already successful platform. The best catalysts I've found to learning and to mastery are observation and mentoring.

I had a profound learning experience regarding this when I went to the Miraval Resort to study with Wyatt Webb, the master equine-assisted learning specialist. He was the main reason I went to attend his workshop—because I considered him the original guru in this type of work. He'd been doing it for decades, he was in his 70s at the time, and I wanted to go before that was no longer an option. I spent a lot of money on the workshop as well as on the mandatory expensive lodging because I wanted to see how the master did it and what I thought would work for me. I went as both a participant and an observer. I went to get good ideas and see what I might need to adjust.

In addition, I made the trip to ask the master if he would mentor me. Ironically, during the workshop, it became glaringly apparent that I had trouble asking for help. To make it worse, I'd put Wyatt on such a pedestal, my usual reticence was compounded exponentially. I put off my question until the workshop was winding down, and it was the "now or never" moment.

Here's how the conversation went. I said, "So, Wyatt... I've got a question for you." In typical Wyatt fashion, he just waited for me to continue. I pressed on. "I was wondering if you would mentor me as an equine-assisted therapy facilitator," I asked. "Nope," he said.

At first, I thought he was kidding because he had just helped me through a lot of my issues around asking for help. Now I was asking him for help, and he wasn't amenable to that? When I realized he wasn't joking, I felt rejected and hurt (because of the story I immediately concocted about what that meant). After I unraveled that,

I asked him why. He told me that he had had some less than favorable experiences with mentoring in the past and that at this point in his life, he didn't want to spend his time that way.

Now, was I disappointed? Immensely. But guess what? In some ways, it didn't matter that he said no. I was forever changed for the **better** just by having asked the question. And in some ways it was actually better that he said no, because I learned so much from that exchange. I learned that I had that level of bravery in me and that, if I worked up the courage to seek out a potential mentor and they declined, it wasn't the end of the world. I also learned not to make up stories about the other person's reasoning and that there are plenty of other ways to learn from someone besides direct mentoring. Wyatt had written a couple of books, and I had just absorbed a ton from observing how he conducted sessions. Ultimately, I learned that there are always other teachers and plenty of other channels of learning.

Which brings me to my next point. We are so incredibly blessed to live in the times we do when you can literally learn almost anything you want over the internet. We have unprecedented access to teachers and lessons which is such an incredible gift. Is it the same as being able to actually interact with a teacher, ask questions, and get immediate answers? Maybe not, but in some ways it can be better. Not having that "advantage" creates space for creativity and experimentation on our part, plus we're not starting out completely blind.

You might think it's not possible to learn from somebody who is already successful because what you are endeavoring to do is novel, perhaps downright revolutionary.

Then we can pose the other question, *Is there anyone who has done this (or something like this, or a part of this) before?*

During my instruction at the Parelli Natural Horsemanship Center, one of the many amazing concepts I was taught was to separate, isolate, and recombine. This technique can be extrapolated to many situations. Even when (or maybe especially when) a goal is unprecedented, we can still break it down into its elements. What other items, services, approaches, or concepts is it similar to? Now separate, isolate, and recombine those elements. Most of the time, that's all ingenuity comes down to anyway.

YOUR TURN

First and foremost, take note of your own successes. If you are reading or listening to this, I guarantee you have many. Really let them sink in and identify every quality you possess that allowed you to be successful in those endeavors and that indicate you will be successful in future goals.

When you're looking to learn or accomplish something new, research who is already successful in this space and see what you can learn from them, whether that's in person, in some sort of apprentice role, or through their books or other media content.

If what you're trying to do has never been done before, separate, isolate, and recombine the elements of something that already exists in such a way that they may be applicable to your new idea. Avail yourself of any opportunity to learn from others who have already been successful in one or more of the elements. Then have a blast creating your novel gift to the world.

?

◆ *Am I on course?*

This question is crazy important if you intend to get to where you want to go. I realized that this was the single most neglected question in my own life. Without it, it is exponentially harder to achieve your goals because it's so easy to get side-tracked. It never ceases to amaze me how getting even slightly off course in the beginning can result in such a drastically different outcome. It's like what my dad taught me about the difference of one degree on a golf swing. It's not much at impact of the ball, but extend that trajectory out, and boy does it make a difference. We had an important saying in the Parelli Horsemanship Program that, again, can be so easily extrapolated into life in general: "Do less sooner rather than more later."

Author Troy Meeder recounts a related story in his highly recommended book, *Average Joe*. Troy, his dad, and his grandfather were out fishing one day in their small fishing boat. My recollection of the story is that when they set out, it was a gorgeous day, but all of the sudden a huge storm came in when they were too far from shore to see land. They made it back to safety one adjustment, one course correction at a time. His dad would calculate their heading, and then a huge wave would knock them off course. He would recalculate their heading, call out an adjustment to Troy's grandad at the helm who would make the adjustment, and they would continue for a few seconds or maybe a minute until the next wave hit. Little by little, one adjustment at a time, they stayed the course and made it into safe harbor.

Another telling example of the importance of monitoring and correcting your course comes from NASA. When a spacecraft gets off its path (which apparently happens on a regular basis), it needs to be course corrected. If it gets too far off course, the mistake cannot be corrected because it doesn't have enough fuel to make large course corrections. So every week, for the duration of the craft's mission, its location, speed, and the direction of flight are calculated and compared with the intended path. A new vector is computed, the attitude thrusters correct the course, and the main thruster pushes it along the path. That is how it stays on course.

It's also how WE stay on course. The trick is to discern how often you need to monitor and course correct. I used to do it once a year which is completely laughable. I don't know why I thought that was ever going to keep me on course. Since realizing how wholly inadequate that was, I have found that the ideal frequency depends on the difficulty of the goal and how long it's going to take. It seems to be inversely proportional to the amount of effort required and the duration of time necessary to achieve the goal. If I'm excited about it and it's easy, especially when it's new, I don't need to monitor or course correct very often. But if the goal is difficult and requires a lot of effort, or if I've been at it a long time and I'm getting impatient or the grind is beginning to wear on me, I know I need to check in and fix what's off more often. Another clue is that if I check in a couple of times in a row and I haven't made any progress or, heaven forbid, I've regressed, or am farther away from my goal, that's an indication I need to monitor and adjust more often.

YOUR TURN

After you've decided where it is you want to go, what the next steps are, and you've set off on your path, I'd invite you to create a program to monitor your progress and discern whether you need course correction to stay on track. Use that system to get you from where you are to where you want to go. When monitoring, if you notice you're off course quite a bit, consider checking in with yourself more frequently. Making small adjustments more often is much easier and far more effective than making large adjustments less often.

?

• *What if?*

I love this question because it opens the door to unlimited possibilities. It's the question that keeps you from being locked into certain outcomes. It's the question that can move you from a fixed mindset to a growth mindset (as described in the book *Mindset* written by psychology professor Dr. Carol Dweck). The *What if?* question is the quintessential question of discovery and innovation. It's the question of fearlessness and bravery and **action** because if you ask *What if?* and try something, you're going to get feedback, and you can go from there. If you didn't like the outcome, you can again ask, *Okay, what if?* and try something else. Or, if you did like the outcome, but want to improve on that, you can again ask *What if?* and try something new that will give you more feedback.

The question itself—the very nature of it—is exploratory. And the nature of exploration is to analyze the discovery and the feedback you received. It virtually eradicates the fear of failure because the result is not something that is **intended** or **expected**. You aren't trying to predetermine the outcome. You're simply experimenting to see what happens, what the outcome IS, rather than what you would have it be. It is a very freeing experience.

You are guided by the actual results instead of your evaluation of whether the results were good or bad, or right or wrong, as compared to your expectations. The results just are what they are and you can decide which "what if" to try next based on those results, or completely independently of them, or to let them go entirely.

I first became aware of the power of this question at the Parelli Natural Horsemanship Center in the spring of 2008. We were discussing different ways people learn. I anticipated they would talk about how some people are visual learners, others auditory, and still others kinesthetic. But instead they explained that some people are "what" learners, some "how" learners, some "why" learners and some "what if" learners.

I remember almost recoiling from the thought of being a "what if" learner at that time. I preferred to be spoon-fed and told the answers and have the "why" explained to me. I hated the idea of having to try to "figure it out," probably because I anticipated meeting with failure many times before I got the desired result and I had a ridiculously low frustration threshold. But what happened was amazing. I'd try something, and the result gave me more information. Then I'd try something else, and that provided more information and so on. At some point, I had accumulated enough information to know how to create a desired result. And along the way, I'd acquired information that could be extrapolated and serve me in ways that had nothing to do with what I was trying to accomplish at that moment. As a byproduct of asking this question repeatedly, I was creating a toolkit (or as we said, a quiver of arrows) that would assist me in addressing future challenges.

Ironically, a huge benefit of the *What if?* question is that it can also be used to achieve an intended goal, by asking *What if?* **until** you get the goal. When you finally achieve that goal, you can relish the rush of accomplishment after effort.

That happened to me later in the day when I experienced a huge real-life lesson while having a play session with my one-year-old horse. The idea was to ask your horse to walk through an obstacle called the car wash. Picture two telephone poles about 10 feet apart with a beam across the top. Streaming down from the beam were long, four-inch-wide clear plastic strips like the kind you sometimes drive through in an actual car wash. To walk through those flapping plastic strips would be hugely traumatic for many horses. And my baby horse was terrified.

I kept asking him to go through over and over, but he was having none of it. I was getting super frustrated when an instructor rode by and told me that, if I forced him through it, I would do damage to the trust between us. She said the idea was to hold him **at** threshold, not push him through it, and let **him** decide when he was ready. Since this was new for me, I wasn't sure what holding him at threshold really meant, so I started playing *What if?* I finally figured out what that meant for him, and ultimately he made the choice to go through on his own. It was incredibly rewarding!

Another real-life example when *What if?* worked for me was when I was trying to participate in a Facebook Live event. As I've said, I am a huge fan of the internet show *Impact Theory*. The host also regularly held live webcasts. I had difficulty connecting to the live sessions and had to watch a couple shows after the fact via a link the staff sent me which prevented me from being able to ask questions during the live event. I was absolutely driven to figure out how to connect to the live show since I wanted in the worst way to participate in the unfolding of the content in real time.

Every Monday, Wednesday and Friday, for the entire hour of the show, I would try to connect. After each "failure," I'd go to Google, get a suggestion, and try that *What if?* When that didn't work, I would go back for another and then another and another. Finally, I had tried everything Google suggested, and nothing worked.

So I started trying my own "what ifs." *What if* I have too much data on my phone, and it can't process the live events anymore? I upgraded my phone. Nope, that wasn't it. *What if* Facebook has the wrong email address for me? I fixed the email on my Facebook account. Nope, that wasn't it. Okay, *What if* my version of Facebook is out of date? I deleted the app from my phone, downloaded it again, and "Voila!" It was a small thing, but the sensation inside was "**victory**!"

The coolest thing was that it reinforced to me that 1) I *can* figure things out if I want them badly enough to be willing to spend the time, and 2) I have the tenacity to keep going until I get my desired result. Don't get me wrong. I'm still a "why" learner too; I still like to be spoon-fed and get the benefit of somebody else's "what ifs" (which can be a powerful springboard for more of your own). But the reality is, the only way they can be **my** wins is if I've played with enough "what ifs" and analyzed the results for myself, for my situation, and for my life.

YOUR TURN

How can you incorporate *What If?* into your life? How might it free you up to experiment and find out what works and what doesn't without fear of self-recrimination? How might it sidestep analysis paralysis? How might it facilitate the acquisition of new skills or polish up existing ones?

This question can be the impetus to get unstuck, change your perspective or mental patterns, think outside the proverbial box, to figure something out, or just to play. "What if" you tried it right now? "What if" it became a regular part of your life?

4

Self-Transcendence

I believe our development as human beings—if done well—takes us from dependence to independence to interdependence. There are many pitfalls and minefields to navigate along the way, and sometimes people don't effectively make the transition from one stage to the next, but, when we do, we definitely shine. In my opinion, human beings are at their absolute highest and best when they are in service to one another.

This section, and the questions in it, can elevate our lives by going beyond the self to contribute to the well-being of others. Self-transcendence is about stepping out of our own lives, and moving toward the very best version of ourselves where we pay it back, or pay it forward, add value to other people's lives, and live in service.

The irony is that when we are able to actually transcend the self, one of the natural consequences is that we are refined and polished into the finest version of ourselves in the process.

?

+ *How can I use this for good?*

This question is instrumental in beginning to consciously live a life of contribution. It can be used to share both the "good" and "bad" in your life so that they might benefit others. The question lends perspective to what you've learned or accomplished that somebody else might find valuable. It's also incredible for getting through adversity as unscathed as possible because it is the silver lining question—it puts pain to a purpose.

There are so many powerful, real-life examples of people who have demonstrated how to answer this question. For me, they epitomize the resilience of the human spirit. They take their tragedy-to-victory stories and hold them up as beacons of light and inspiration to others. They are like the Phoenix rising out of the ashes—everyday heroes and heroines who live among us, scraped-up, battle-weary and scarred, but they've transformed what they lived through into a resolution to thrive and inspire others to do the same.

One woman who made such an impact on my life was Immaculée Ilibagiza, author of an incredible memoir, *Left to Tell*. Immaculée survived the 1994 Rwandan holocaust by hiding for 91 days with seven other women in a three-foot-by-four-foot bathroom in the home of a local pastor. While she was in hiding, she could hear the taunting of the "soldiers" who were hunting her to kill her. They had already murdered the rest of her family except one brother who was out of the country. She was finally rescued, weighing only 65 pounds. After everything she endured, when she faced one of the men responsible for killing her family, instead of being consumed by rage and hate as many would have been, she treated him with compassion and forgiveness. After processing the horrors of what had happened to her, she sought out and provided support to other orphans of the holocaust. She emigrated from Rwanda to the United States, worked at the United Nations, married, and had two children. Today she is a full-time inspirational speaker, author, producer, and director. She took one of the most horrific tragedies imaginable—civil war that left her country in ruins, her life in complete chaos, and her family members hacked to death by machetes—and turned it for good. I had the privilege of attending one of her talks. As soon as she walked into the room, I started to cry from the intensity and beauty of her presence. Her spirit was purified by fire, and it was palpable.

If we're to get the most out of the *How can I use this for good?* question, I think the trick is to minimize the time between the triggering event and when you ask the question. It still works to do it later, and it's certainly better to do it later than not at all. (In fact, this question can shift crusty, old hurts that have calcified into bitterness.) But I believe our joys can be magnified and our adverse experiences lightened commensurately with how quickly we ask this question.

The irritation with a co-parent who constantly makes life difficult can be eased when that pain is channeled to create a closer bond with your children. The grit required to go through the diagnosis and treatment of a serious illness can become a poignant reminder to live each day of life more fully, to relish so many moments you would have missed before, and articulate and demonstrate your affection for friends and family you may have been taking for granted. The loss of someone dearly loved can be mitigated, however slightly, by honoring their memory by living well and serving others. Pain with a purpose is very different from abject suffering.

While life can be improved by asking this question in the midst of struggle, sometimes we just can't find a silver lining when we're eyeball deep in the muck and mire. If we keep asking it—even well after the fact—the answer is likely to become clear at some point. With it, the relief of releasing anguish or bitterness that had a hold on you will arrive.

Suffering that has not been born in vain is more palatable, even noble. When you meet the suffering head-on, and not only refuse to let it take you down, but actually transmute it to be used for good, is when you get to experience the full radiance of your own Spirit.

YOUR TURN

I'd invite you to consider this question whenever you encounter a challenging time or event in your life. My personal philosophy/mission statement is "Learn. Grow. Share. Encourage. Repeat." So whenever you experience something worth sharing, it's a good time to ask *How can I use this for good?* And any time you come through a struggle, you overcome an obstacle, or you overtake adversity, you have something worth sharing. Even, and maybe especially, in the midst of your trials, asking *How can I use this for good?* will give a purpose to your pain. That purpose can make all the difference.

108

?

• *How can I use my gifts/talents/skills to serve others?*

This question is similar to the previous one, but instead of converting your life experiences into contributions to the well-being of others, we ask how specific talents we were gifted with, or skills we've developed, can be applied in service.

This question created one of the biggest turnarounds in my life. I was working in yet another law firm, but this one was by far the darkest. In addition to the already high-pressure environment of law, upper management was elitist and stiflingly controlling, and middle management suffered from constant turnover—five office managers in four years, each one crazier than the last. The culture was the ultimate in fixed mindset; people were gossipy, openly hostile, and constantly looking for someone to blame or throw under the bus.

It's difficult to express how much I dreaded going to work every day. The only thing that kept me coming back was that I was fortunate enough to support the two nicest lawyers in the office—both exceptionally kind human beings—but the bulk of every day was still miserable because of the toxic and highly dysfunctional culture. And it felt like it was getting worse with every moment.

Fortunately, one of my "extracurricular" activities at the time involved my church. I was part of the leadership team, and we had the privilege of participating in a training to help us recognize our "gifts." During that process, the gift of being an "encourager" was identified. I lit up like a Christmas tree, because I completely resonated with that single-word description of what I considered my core mission. Now that I knew what my gift was, I could ask the question *How can I use it to serve others?*

Spiritual leader Marianne Williamson talked about the concept of tending your corner of the garden in a lecture I attended. I'm paraphrasing here, but the gist of it was that, if you didn't care for and nurture the area you were given, you weren't going to be given a bigger piece (or a better garden for that matter!). I realized that tending my "corner of the garden" meant that I needed to live my mission—encouraging—**regardless** of the environment I was in. To call on another garden metaphor, I needed to effectively "bloom where I was planted."

I'd heard life coach Marie Forleo talk about living your passion contemporaneously **while** you're working your "day job," and it suddenly hit me that this was not an either/or situation. It's an AND situation. I could be who I was meant to be and share my gifts in the job I was in **AND** work toward moving into a job that was more fully aligned with who I am.

I started viewing my job as a mission field, a playground, and a training program. My job became a place where I could serve others by encouraging the people I worked with. I shared things that were meant to uplift, to inspire, to shift and reconnect them with their highest and best **in the midst of** our regular, corporate day jobs. There were many opportunities in that environment (as there are in any environment) to practice *with* others AND *on* myself. I began to hone my skills and sharpen iron with iron—to experiment with what worked and what didn't. Instead of waiting until I actually stepped into a coaching position to be an encourager, I decided to transform fully into who I was where I was. It was crazy how quickly things changed. Shortly after I shifted my focus to how I could use my gifts to serve people in my workplace, all of the high drama people either quit or were let go, and I was no longer upset and agitated on a regular basis. A few months later, my nice lawyers and I moved to a new firm that was a 180-degree turn from the previous one. The people were professional, kind, and team oriented. And it wasn't just rhetoric. Even more importantly, my boss told me that, while I was good at my job, my real value to him was that I lifted him up when he felt beaten up by the world. Pretty incredible affirmation and a wonderful reward for asking the question *How can I use my gifts/talents/skills to serve others?* and living out the answer.

YOUR TURN

Multi-passionate, highly successful entrepreneur Marie Forleo has an inspirational tagline that says "because the world needs that special gift that only you have to offer." What is that gift, or talent, or skill only you have to offer? Is it a unique ability or is it maybe that just the **way** you do it is what makes it special? Likely the older you get, the more you will have to offer. Once you've discerned what your special gift is, it's time to ask the question *How can I use it to serve others?* and watch the magic unfold. It's an incredible win-win because it's difficult, if not impossible, to watch somebody else benefit from something you contributed to them and not feel pretty darn good about it.

?

- *How can I enhance one of my relationships today?*

I love this question because it makes sure you aren't neglecting a relationship that is important to you.

Stephen Covey is most famous for his book, *7 Habits of Highly Effective People*, but he also wrote one called *First Things First* that I think is every bit as important, if not more so. In it he takes you through a remarkable process that sets you up well for feeling a lot more satisfaction and the closest thing I've found to a balanced life.

First, you list the five to six most important roles you fill in your life. For example, mine are daughter, sister, dog mom, employee, coach, and CALROCK Ranch developer. Then, each week, you review your calendar and determine where you can schedule things that will enhance that role or relationship. His system takes into consideration that some weeks (or longer time periods) will necessarily be out of balance. Maybe there's a particularly time-consuming project at work, or maybe you're caring for an ailing parent. For those weeks or for that period of time, you can't schedule as many relationship-enhancing activities or moments. Ideally, when life comes back into relative balance for a while (since it's never in balance permanently), you can add more of them in.

What's particularly eye-opening about this method is that it keeps you aware of roles or relationships you might be neglecting. If a few weeks go by and I haven't done anything with my sisters, I'm more aware of that as a result of the system. That awareness creates opportunities to rectify the situation before too much time goes by and it's harder to fix. What's also eye-opening is another section called "Sharpen the Saw" where you schedule self-care activities so you don't neglect your own needs and find yourself depleted.

My sister also does a lovely thing related to this question. She picks somebody she wants to feel special that day and takes steps to give that gift to them. She's done things like cover her kids' doors with Post-it notes that each say something she loves about them. She's sent me flowers more than once when I was going through a tough time. She recreated a tradition we had when we were kids called "Bookstahootie" which is a surprise outing for your loved ones. She restarted the tradition with an evening at her house when my mom, my other sister, and I each got a personalized wine glass which we filled and toasted with. Then we went to dinner and a theatrical presentation of the *Rocky Horror Picture Show* where we got to meet the cast afterward. She's done countless selfless, generous things to make her loved ones feel special. She's also learned that it's a particularly effective remedy to lift herself out of the doldrums because it's a big win-win. She always says, "When you're down, do something for somebody else." Doing something relationship-enhancing keeps you in touch with what and who is good in this life.

YOUR TURN

Which are the relationships that mean the most to you? What can do you to enhance one of those today? One of the main determinants of the quality of life experienced by human beings is the quality of their relationships. If you ask yourself this question every day and execute on the answer you come up with, your life and your self-concept will be immeasurably enriched. So where will you start?

?

- *How can I leave the world a little (or a lot) better than I found it?*

This is another appropriate question for self-transcendence because it focuses us on contribution and something larger than ourselves. This is an opportunity to devote yourself to making a difference in big and small ways as there are many, many ways to leave the world a better place. Whether it's sharing something you have, teaching something you've learned, providing someone with something they need, creating something beautiful or helpful, there are literally limitless ways that can enhance someone else's life and/or the places we live. They can range from simple to elaborate, from free to very expensive, but I believe it's the intention behind our action or avenue that actually leaves the world a better place. This question orients our lives toward practicing kindness and spreading goodness. It is the very substance of a fulfilling life.

The "random act of kindness" movement called attention to this idea or question very effectively, but I think even more powerful is when we practice **intentional** acts of kindness. Here there are also tremendous win-wins. My mom and I used to go to dinner and have a blast picking out a table of people whose check we were going to pick up. Or I loved paying the toll for the person behind me on my morning commute. I loved imagining how we might have left their day just a little bit better than it would otherwise have been. The point is, it doesn't take much—sometimes even holding the door open for someone, or giving someone the gift of your smile, or just paying a genuine compliment can really change someone's day.

Sometimes it can change their entire lives. When I was in my 20s, my best friend was involved in an emotionally abusive relationship. Like the "boiling frog in a pot" story, little by little her boyfriend had gradually and completely eroded her self-esteem. She no longer felt her own worth, and she had fallen into a pattern of tolerating inexcusable behavior from him. I was young, so I didn't understand how this could have happened, and I was more than a little incredulous because this woman was phenomenal—inside and out. Not only was she gorgeous, she was generous, kind, warmhearted, family-oriented, successful, savvy, and funny as hell. So I just started pointing out those attributes and how people other than the boyfriend (and, at one point, fiancé!) reacted to her. Bit by bit she regained a clearer perspective and came back to her senses about who she really was and the inherent value she had. As a result, she was no longer willing to tolerate his abusive treatment, and she eventually broke free from his grasp. Decades later, she told me she credited me with saving her life during that time. So you really never know how profound the seemingly smallest of kindnesses can be.

One of the simplest, cheapest, and most impactful ways in which we can leave the world a better place is by becoming conscious about the quality of our attention and where we focus it. It's about becoming more present (something that challenges me every single day!) and giving two of the most precious gifts we have—our time and attention—to the people who cross our path.

In my opinion, it's more important than ever. Especially in the West. We live at warp speed, and much of our interaction with other people is done remotely and digitally. We get near-constant hits of all kinds of neurochemical highs from that kind of "communication," but we are left completely bereft of real, meaningful, face-to-face, human-to-human interaction. I believe the technology in our world is a double-edged sword. It can be incredibly useful. It can be life-enhancing and even life-saving, but it is not a substitute for interpersonal communication and connection. And the lack of quality connection is the root cause of a myriad of intensely destructive problems today—many of which could be remedied, or at least significantly diminished, by the reclamation or addition of quality interpersonal relationships.

I was privileged to witness the power of such a relationship when my mother befriended a sweet young man with a horrible disease. My mom was volunteering at a homeless mission and would go there once a week to offer neck and back massages to the homeless ladies who came there for meals, some of whom had not been touched in years. She became particularly fond of and moved by a young man she met there who suffered from Huntington's disease, a brutal degenerative disorder. As his disease progressed, he was eventually moved into a full-time care facility that was 45 miles from my mother's house. But, for a long time, this little 81-year-old lady drove to that facility every week to visit with him for a couple of hours. She brought games they could play together, she continued to give him neck massages, she would bring decorations for his room each holiday and always gave him his only birthday and Christmas gifts. Even in his deteriorated state, he would light up when my mother walked into the room. For the couple of hours she was there, he would smile and laugh a lot. Even though the drive was hard on her, and it took a lot of energy, it was also a win for her. She knew she was making the world, especially his world, a little better than she found it. To me, there is no better purpose or more noble meaning to our lives.

YOUR TURN

Ironically, this question will leave **your** world better than you found it. It is the prompt to live your most satisfying, fulfilled life by asking yourself how you, in particular, can leave the world a little better than you found it. Who is in need of something you can give? What can you create that might enrich the environment, someone else's day, or even their life? What are you really good at that you can contribute now or in the future? What kind of positive legacy can you leave through those contributions? And how might asking these questions every day change the world?

I invite you to play with this. I can pretty much guarantee that the more you do it, the more you'll want to do it, the more gratifying your own life will be and the more you will leave the world better than you found it. At the end of your time on Earth, it will have been a life well lived.

5

Coming Full Circle

In the end, it turns out sometimes *Why?* actually is a useful question. It brings us back to the beginning because it's an effective question to create self-awareness, and it's also a remarkable question for self-transcendence because it can be used to connect people through a common purpose or mission. So, last but not least, let's take a look at the power of *Why?*

?

- *Why?*

There are two scenarios where I find the *Why?* question extraordinarily useful. The first is during self-examination and getting clarity about your own motivations. As was discussed in the beginning of this book, understanding your patterns can provide the clarity that creates enough space between an agitating event and your reaction so that you can choose your response instead of just reacting reflexively. Repeated, careful examination of why you did something, or said something, or didn't do something, or didn't say something, can allow you to recognize the destructive patterns in your life. That will then afford you the opportunity to change them.

In essence, the benefit of this question is described perfectly in *Autobiography in 5 Short Chapters*, a thought-provoking piece by Portia Nelson:

Chapter I
I walk down the street.
There is a deep hole in the sidewalk.
I fall in.
I am lost...I am helpless.
It isn't my fault.
It takes me forever to find a way out.

Chapter II
I walk down the same street.
There is a deep hole in the sidewalk.

I pretend I don't see it.
I fall in again.
I can't believe I am in the same place.
But it isn't my fault.
It still takes a long time to get out.

Chapter III

I walk down the same street.
There is a deep hole in the sidewalk.
I see it is there.
I fall in...it's a habit.
My eyes are open.
I know where I am.
It is *my* fault.
I get out immediately.

Chapter IV

I walk down the same street.
There is a deep hole in the sidewalk.
I walk around it.

Chapter V

I walk down a different street.

In addition to revealing unproductive thought or behavior patterns, *Why?* can also be used to recognize good/productive/effective patterns in your life, so you can begin to examine how to strengthen and reinforce them.

Finally, *Why?* can be instrumental for clarifying and clearly communicating a mission, as well as for achieving resonance, alignment, and buy-in. Two of my favorite mentors, Tom Bilyeu and Michael Gervais, are exceptionally talented at this. Although they each approach their missions very differently, in the end, they are both interested in seeing people actually take action to create the best version of themselves and a better version of their lives. People who are interested in and value that mission—the people for whom that resonates—find Tom and Mike, they become part of their online communities, they contribute within the community, and it makes for a richer experience for all.

I am about to embark on one of my rest-of-my-life missions of building a ranch that serves girls who have survived sex trafficking and using my coaching skills and life experiences to help facilitate their healing. I am very clear on what I want to do and why I want to do it. I spent a long time dreaming about it, which turned into envisioning and planning and finally communicating that plan. People whose hearts are also broken for those girls are coming out in droves to help me build this ranch and provide hope, resources, and a real chance at a better life for these girls. When you're clear on your "why," the people who are aligned with you and/or your cause will find you. Together you can create something far greater than you could ever do without them. Together everyone transcends themselves for the creation of the greater good. In the process, everyone is enriched and made better.

Your Turn

If you are repeatedly engaging in a mental or behavioral pattern that doesn't serve you, *Why?* can be an extremely useful question in helping you discern and then change your motivations. I challenge you to keep asking the question **until** you get down to the answer that actually facilitates the change you seek.

Another transformative use of *Why?* is to dissect positive mental or behavioral patterns to understand what makes them work so you can extrapolate them to other areas of your life, or identify ways they might be effective for someone else. The invitation here is to examine *Why?* you do some of the positive, beneficial things you do and then to figure out how to expand on or share them.

Finally, get clear on the "why" of your mission, your purpose, or the meaning of your life (or of this period of your life). The distillation of that will anchor and focus you and also serve as a beacon to other like-minded people who will inevitably make the journey a deeper, richer experience.

EPILOGUE

There you have it. It's certainly not an exhaustive list of questions, but these are the core gems I found most useful in transitioning from (or maybe back and forth and between is a better description) self-awareness to self-regulation to self-mastery and ultimately to self-transcendence.

I do not profess to be an expert and am in no way suggesting that the questions will make your life perfect, but as you continue to work with them and progress through them, you should see fewer incidents of negative emotions. During the times when you do experience them, you'll know how to handle them, the intensity will be diminished, the duration will be shorter, and the resolution faster.

As you continue even further through the questions, they will assist you in creating a life you intend, to become more of the person you most want to be, and to contribute to the world in a way only you can. They will keep you on track for experiencing an increasingly deep, fulfilling, rich life.

Or so it has been for me. I have found that the work involved in answering the questions was well worth the effort. The answers have dramatically (albeit slowly) increased my level of peace and satisfaction with life. May it be the same for you.

YOUR TURN

How might these or other "Useful Questions" catapult you to the next, better version or yourself, or help you to exponentially improve the quality of *your* life?...

REFERENCED RESOURCES

PEOPLE

Lisa Bilyeu
@lisabilyeu on Instagram and Facebook

Tom Bilyeu
https://en.wikipedia.org/wiki/Thomas_Bilyeu
www.impacttheory.com

Jack Canfield
www.jackcanfield.com

Stephen Covey
https://en.wikipedia.org/wiki/Stephen_Covey

Carol Dweck, Ph.D.
https://en.wikipedia.org/wiki/Carol_Dweck

Marie Forleo
www.marieforleo.com
www.marietv.com

Michael Gervais, Ph.D.
www.findingmastery.net

www.competetocreate.net
https://www.linkedin.com/in/drmichaelgervais

David Goggins
www.davidgoggins.com

Immaculée Ilibagiza
https://en.wikipedia.org/wiki/Immacul%C3%A9e_ Ilibagiza

Byron Katie
www.thework.com

Troy Meeder
www.crystalpeaksyouthranch.org

Topher Morrison, Ph.D.
www.tophermorrison.com

Christopher J. Mruk, Ph.D.
https://cmruk.org

Cheryl Richardson
www.cherylrichardson.com

Tony Robbins
www.tonyrobbins .com

Jim Rohn
www.jimrohn.com

David Foster Wallace
https://en.wikipedia.org/wiki/David_Foster_Wallhttpsv

Wyatt Webb
https://en.wikipedia.org/wiki/Wyatt_Webb
https://www.miravalarizona.com/experiences/explore/
specialists-2/wyatt-webb

Marianne Williamson
www.marianne.com